# いのち綾なす
## インド北東部への旅

Weaving of Spirit:
A Journey into
North East India

延江由美子
Yumiko Nobue

私をいつもあたたかく受け入れてくださったインド北東部の人々と、
この素晴らしい地域での奉仕に献身してきたシスターたちに、
心からの感謝と友愛を込めて。

With deep gratitude and affection
to the peoples of North East India who have always
welcomed me wholeheartedly into their lives,
and to our Sisters who have dedicated themselves
to the mission in this beautiful land.

# はじめに

今でも「知られざる」という形容詞がぴったりなインド北東部。インドの他の州とは鶏の首にたとえられる細い部分でわずかにつながっているのみで、ほとんどの領域がネパール、ブータン、チベット、ミャンマー、そしてバングラデシュに接しています。中心部には大河ブラマプトラ川が流れる平野が広がり、周辺地域は山岳地で豊かな自然に恵まれています。そこにはそれぞれに独自の言語や生活風習を持つ数多くの民族が住んでおり、彼らの顔立ちはいわゆるインド人というよりも、東南アジア人か東アジア人の佇まいです。

私はローマ・カトリック教会の女子修道会メディカル・ミッション・シスターズ（MMS）の一員として、2007年からこの地で活動してきました。当初から、見るもの、聞くもの、食べるもの、どれもこれもが新鮮で驚くことばかり。もともと写真が好きな私はいつも小さなデジカメを持ち歩き、ことあるごとに撮っていました。それらをまとめたのが1冊目の写真集『Moving Cloud Flowing Water: A Journey Into North East India』（邦題＝行雲流水──インド北東部への旅、2015年）です。

ここ数年、私の主な役目は召命勧誘（修道生活を希望する高校生に会い、連絡を取り合うこと）と、私たちの修道院に寄宿す

る生徒たちに寄り添いながら指導することです。私はここインド北東部出身者のような顔立ちで、年齢は生徒たちにとっては伯母、若いシスターたちにとっては年長のお姉さんくらい、文化的にはアジア人だけど欧米を含め多様な異文化生活も体験している、というわけで、どうやらこの仕事に適しているようです。おかげで現地の人々と親しく交わる機会が増え、活動範囲も少しずつ広がりました。10年以上経った今も、日々出会う人々のたくましさや生き生きとした子どもたちの姿に感動し、どこか懐かしい田園風景にほっと気持ちが和らぎます。しかしその一方で、非常に複雑でセンシティブな歴史的背景と現実があることもだんだんとわかってきました。

私にとっていろいろな意味で特別なインド北東部の素晴らしさをより具体的に伝えられるよう、2冊目となる『いのち綾なす──インド北東部への旅』には、MMSとしての活動を通して、興味を掻き立てられたり美しいと感じたりした日常生活の風景に加えて、印象的だった見聞や言い伝えなどを収めました。私は修道者として、文化や宗教や国籍や性別の違いといった諸々の境界を越える橋渡しのような存在になれたらいいなと願っています。日本家屋には「縁側」という、「外と内」「人と人」をつなぐスペースがあります。このささやかな作品が縁側のように、未知でいてなぜか馴染みのあるインド北東部とのご縁を結ぶ空間となり、そこに住む人々と私たち一人一人をつなぐきっかけとなれば望外の喜びです。

# Introduction

The region of North East India is considered as an unknown part of the world still today. A very narrow corridor links it to the rest of India. Nepal, Bhutan, Tibet, Myanmar and Bangladesh encircle most of the area. Consisting of vast plains spread along the Brahmaputra River, while also being surrounded by mountains, the North East is geographically diverse and holds many riches. Over the centuries, numerous tribes with unique cultures have lived side by side in this area. Interestingly, their features and the cultures are quite different from those of other parts of India.

Medical Mission Sisters (MMS) is an international congregation of women religious of the Roman Catholic Church. In 2007 I joined our sisters in North East India, and from the beginning, I was fascinated by almost everything I encountered. Being already fond of photography, I always carried a small digital camera wherever I went. Eventually, from the growing photo journal I had, a pictorial memoir evolved, *Moving Cloud Flowing Water: A Journey Into North East India*, which was published in 2015.

In recent years my main task is vocation promotion and accompaniment of the students who stay with us in our convent. It seems it is a good match. I do look like a native of North East India, about the age of their parents' elder sister, and am an Asian who has various cross-cultural experiences including the West. Over the years the area of my involvement has gradually widened and the work with which I have been entrusted has given me many opportunities to get to know different peoples in the region. Even now after more than ten years, I admire their stamina and toughness, remain captivated by the children's ever vibrant expression and continue to discover the treasures of their cultures. The rural landscape reminds me of countryside in Japan and makes me feel at ease. Gradually I become aware of the historical background and contemporary realities which are immensely complex and sensitive. My understanding is growing with reading and study and keeping notes of what people share with me – and there is so much more to learn!

In so many ways, the region of North East India is a very special place for me and I love to share the beauty and diversity with wider communities. In the book are scenes and tales that have stirred me during our day-to-day life in mission. As a religious, I wish to be a bridge going beyond boundaries of culture, religion, race, nationality, and gender. In a traditional Japanese house, there is a particular structure called *engawa*, literally meaning edge and side. It connects outside and inside: in a way it is considered as both. Around *engawa*, people simply enjoy each other's company. Sometimes a new relationship emerges among people and sometimes a discovery comes forth from casual conversations. It is my hope that just like *engawa* this humble photo book would be a hospitable space inviting you to encounter the unknown and yet somewhat familiar world of North East India, creating a connection between you and the peoples there. May it be so.

# Weaving of Spirit
## A Journey into
## North East India

いのち綾なす　インド北東部への旅

延江由美子
Yumiko Nobue

# 目次
## Contents

# 道標
<ruby>道<rt>みち</rt></ruby><ruby>標<rt>しるべ</rt></ruby>

マリア・ホーナング
MMS会員、『他宗教との出会い』(2007年)著者

私が著者である延江由美子に初めて会ったのは1990年代
初頭。彼女が持つ、世界のどこにでも居場所を見つけるこ
とができる柔軟性と、いつも自然体で人と触れ合う振る舞
いには大いに感心したものです。ほどなくして彼女と私はメ
ディカル・ミッション・シスターズ(MMS)の創立者、アンナ・デ
ンゲルが目指した癒やしの道を共に歩むことになりました。

2007年にインド北東部のミッションに携わるようになるまで、
由美子はフィリピン、マラウイ、アメリカ合衆国、イギリス、日
本、インドで生活し、奉仕してきました。それぞれの土地の
文化を身につけながら溶け込んでいった体験が、この写真
集出版の原動力です。
現地の文化を丸ごと受け入れる包容力、異なる価値観や倫
理観を理解しようとする心、それぞれの人生が醸し出す趣
きや深い意味を捉える感受性。彼女が持ち合わせているこ
うした素質が、人々とのつながりを容易にしているのだと思
います。由美子の美的センスは、彼女を育んだ日本文化と
その人柄から表れているのでしょう。生きることの美しさと
哀しみを慈しむ天賦の才能が、写真からも文章からも感じ
られます。
1冊目の写真集『Moving Cloud Flowing Water: A Journey
Into North East India』(邦題=行雲流水──インド北東部への旅、
2015年)が表現する、たくましい生命力と独創性に溢れすべ
てを包み込むような世界観に私の想像力は大いに刺激さ

れました。この2冊目『いのち綾なす──インド北東部への旅』にはさらに計り知れない展開があると期待しています。

アジア人であることで由美子はインド北東部の風景にすっと溶け込み、現地出身者だと見なされます。この本は再び、そんな彼女が辿ってきたユニークな旅へと私たちを誘います。現地の人々にすっかり魅了された彼女は、自分の目で見て心で感じたことを他の人たちにも見てほしいと熱く強く思っているのです。

この本で紹介されるのは、過去、現在、そして未来が同時に人々の中で力強く鼓動し、そこに住む人々からは明確なアイデンティティが自然と滲み出ている、今となっては数少ない土地です。日々変わりゆく世界の流れの中で、彼らの文化や社会はこれから一体どうなっていくのでしょうか。人々と「行き」、目の前に展開するそのものと「流れ」ようと真摯に心がける彼女が切り取った風景を見ながらそう思わずにいられません。というのも、これはインド北東部に限ったことではなく、今私たちが直面している人類共通の現実だからです。

より良い世界を築いていくためには、私たち市民同士、そして国同士がつながり一致することが欠かせないという意識が今、人々の間で確実に広まっています。新型コロナウイルスや人種差別などが拡大する中で、国内外の共通善実現に向けた探究が進んでいき、アントニオ・グテーレス国連事務総長や教皇フランシスコはこれと同じことを、地球規模の視野を持って表現しています。

グテーレス国連事務総長は2021年1月、各国首脳に向けて「今後やってくる試練を乗り越えるためにはより包括的でより緊密な多国間連携が求められることは明らかです。〔…〕死から健康へ、災害から復興へ、絶望から希望へ、いつもと変わらない作業から改革へと、私たちは方向転換しなければならないのです」「過去の過ちを正し、現在の構造的不正に取り組むべき時です」と語りました。彼は演説の中で

「私たちは必ず成し遂げねばならないのです。共に」と繰り返し訴えています。

教皇フランシスコは、「フラテッリ・トゥッティ（兄弟の皆さん）」と題された兄弟愛と社会的友愛をテーマにした回勅で次のように述べています。「私は、一人一人の尊厳を認めることで、私たちが生きている今この時代に兄弟愛への普遍的な憧れを甦らせたいと心から願っています。男女の区別なく、すべての人に対する友愛です」「［イエスの福音は］夢を持ち、この生を素晴らしい冒険にする道を示しています。一人で生きることなど誰にもできません。［…］支え助けてくれる仲間、前を見ながら助け合い歩み続けることができる共同体が必要なのです」「共に夢見る。なんと大切なことでしょうか。さあ、一緒に夢を描きましょう。同じ人間の家族として、旅の同伴者として、私たちが共に暮らす家であるこの地球の子どもとして。一人一人が自分の信仰や信念という富を持ち寄り、自分の声で夢を語りましょう、兄弟姉妹として」。

MMSは2022年に開かれる国際会議を準備するにあたり、それぞれの場所で今日のミッションのあり方について、「私たちは分断された世界に癒やしをもたらし一つになろうと、グローバルな多文化共同体として心を合わせ一致していく使命が与えられている」と考えています。そして、私たち各々が人類という家族の一員だと信じるのなら、「信念を体現し、理想とする一致を育み、支え、広めていくために必要なことを行う」ことを目指しているのです。私たちが起こすべき行動は広範囲に及びますが、この『いのち綾なす』はまさにその一つと言えるでしょう。

人類共同体が持つ洞察力と創造力の可能性は、たとえば延江由美子さんのような人が何かの形で示さなければ、暗闇の中に隠されたままになってしまいます。今こそ、すべての被造物の繁栄と正義と平和のために私たちが共に努力することが持つ可能性を高らかに表明すべき時だと思います。そして、この本は確かにそれをうたいあげているのです。

# Invitation

Maria Hornung

Medical Mission Sisters,
author of *Encountering Other Faiths* (2007)

I first met the author, Yumiko Nobue in the early 1990's.
My overwhelming impression was of a woman whose home
is the world. I so admired the ease with which this Japanese
woman engaged the many encounters she had with others.
Yumiko and I embarked on the spiritual journey of following
the healing charism of Anna Dengel, founder of the international Congregation of Medical Mission Sisters.

Over the years Yumiko has lived and ministered in the
Philippines, Malawi, the United States and England as well
as Japan and India. In 2007, Yumiko became involved in our
mission in North East India. It is Yumiko's enculturation
into the life and ways of the people that has empowered her
to engage this project of creating and making public her
pictorial memoirs.
Yumiko has an open embrace of culture; understanding of
operational values and ethics; and sensitivity to artistic and
personal expressions of life's beauty and deep meanings.
Because of this, people easily bond with her. Yumiko's artistic capabilities are part of her personal and cultural heritage.
Whether in writings or photo art, all seems to be done
with a God-given talent to cherish the beauty and pathos
of human life.
One of the things that has thrilled me in reading her first
book, *Moving Cloud, Flowing Water: A Journey Into North
East India* is that it has opened me to a worldview that feeds
my imagination with its vitality, ingenuity and inclusivity.
I look forward to even more in her new book, *Weaving of
Spirit: A Journey into North East India.*
We are again invited into a unique piece of her journey.
Because of her ethnic background and physical features

Yumiko blends into the tribal landscape and is perceived as one of their own. Having been captivated by the peoples of North East India, Yumiko has a passion for wanting others to glimpse for themselves what her eyes and heart have seen and felt.

This second book aims to deepen our acquaintance with several peoples in the region of North East India. Her passion and commitment in "moving" with the people and "flowing" with unfolding realities impels us to discover beauty and meaning as well as challenge and opportunity. There are now precious few places on earth where the evidence of past, present and future beat strong among people, engendering an identity with clear characteristics and deep meaning. What does the evolving future hold for such vibrant peoples, cultures and social constructs? In such a book as *Weaving of Spirit*, you can enter that reality — one that has, in fact, belonged to all human communities.

It is truly a book for our times as we search for connectedness among the members of the human family. There is now a growing universal human consciousness of the utterly essential need for connectedness among peoples and nations as the greatest requirement for betterment of the world. The words of Antonio Guterres, Secretary General of the United Nations and Pope Francis articulate this in global terms amidst our pandemics of the corona virus, racism, and the search for constructive ways to work for the common good in nations and globally.

Guterres spoke to the heads of nations in January 2021, "The challenges ahead clearly demand a more inclusive and more networked multilateralism... We need to move from death to health; from disaster to reconstruction; from despair to hope; from business as usual to transformation." "It is time to redress the wrongs of the past and address the systemic injustices of our time." Repeatedly, throughout his message, Guterres said, "We must make it happen. Together." Pope Francis in his encyclical, *Fratelli Tutti*, says, "It is my desire that, in this our time, by acknowledging the dignity of each human person, we can contribute to the rebirth of a universal aspiration to fraternity. Fraternity between all men and women." The essential Gospel message "...shows us how to dream and to turn our life into a wonderful adventure.

No one can face life in isolation... We need a community that supports and helps us, in which we can help one another to keep looking ahead."

"How important it is to dream together... Let us dream, then, as a single human family, as fellow travelers sharing the same flesh, as children of the same earth which is our common home, each of us bringing the richness of his or her beliefs and convictions, each of us with his or her own voice, brothers and sisters all."

As Medical Mission Sisters prepare for their international convocation in 2022, they name the Chapter's theme of discerning mission today as, "We are called to become one as an inter-cultural body with a global mission to promote healing and wholeness in a divided world." If we believe that we are all part of one human family, "...we will live out of that belief and do what it takes to nurture, support and further create the oneness we desire."

*Weaving of Spirit* is an essential part of our Congregation — wide response to promote oneness among peoples for the healing of the nations.

The vision and creative potential of what the human community is capable of is left hidden in the darkness without the witness of amazing human beings such as Nobue Yumiko san. Now, more than ever, the potential of humans working together for ensuring prosperity and justice and peace for all needs to be spoken loudly and clearly. And in this book, it surely is.

# インド北東部における
# メディカル・ミッション・シスターズの活動の歩み

レティチア・エアルテイル［原文］
延江由美子［翻訳・編集］


1967年、アッサム州ディブルガール教区の司教からメディカル・ミッション・シスターズ（MMS）に、ナガランド州の州都コヒマに病院を建て医療活動を開始するよう要請がありました。最初の調査で医療面のニーズは甚大と判断され、さらなる調査の結果、MMSはコヒマに住むアンガミ・ナガ族を対象としたミッションを決定し、1970年に政府と共同して3人のシスターによる医療活動が始まったのです。政府からは診療所と移動診療車として使えるジープが提供され、年に一度の助成金も支給されました。周囲60キロメートル圏内をジープで回り、ミッションは順調に進んでいきました。そして、地元の人々が自分たちで管理できるようにと、村ごとに保健師を養成しました。

第2のミッションの地は、メガラヤ州トゥラ教区ガロヒルズです。インド南部ケララ州のMMSをよく知っている神父からの依頼で、1972年にケララ州出身の4人のシスターが東ガロヒルズ（現北ガロヒルズ）メンディパタに建てられた小さな診療所に派遣されます。精力的に行われた村への訪問は、シスターがガロ族の言葉や生活習慣、文化を学び、人々と親しくなるための第一歩となりました。また診療所での活動に加えて、健康、農業、社会経済福祉などに関わるプロジェクトを企画し、人々の意識向上を図りました。1998年にはゴム生産者のための生協を立ち上げ、その後大いに発展し、地域社会に貢献してきました。今でも政府によるプログラム

を含む様々な活動を主導しています。

第3のミッションの地は、トゥラ教区西ガロヒルズにあるラジャバラ村です。1976年に同じくケララ州出身の4人のシスターによって始まりました。MMSの修道院は、社会医療センターとして生活のあらゆる面で人々の大きな支えとなっていきます。ここでは学童保育も活発で、またMMSの訓練を受けた保健師たちは地域の医療活動にとってなくてはならない存在になりました。MMSが現地入りして20年後には教会もでき、今でもカトリック共同体の基盤です。

第4のミッションの地は、ナガランド州チュムケディマです。1993年に3人のシスターが派遣され、コヒマ教区とMMSが共同して、薬物とアルコール中毒者のためのリハビリセンターを開きました。それと同時に、MMSへの召命の推進を目的とした学生寮を始めることが司教から許可されたのです。現在、チュムケディマの修道院は北東部管区の養成所でもあり、教会だけでなく地域での様々な活動に参加しています。

2005年には地理的な利便性も考慮し、アッサム州ボンガイガオン教区での第5のミッションが始まりました。修道院の近隣には様々なエスニックグループの人々が住んでおり、医療に加えて、女性の地位向上、学童保育や家庭訪問など、地域に密着した幅広い活動を展開しています。

第1のミッションが開始されてから2020年で半世紀を迎え、異なる民族的・文化的背景を持つインド北東部出身の会員も徐々に増えてきました。長年にわたってインド北東部でのミッションに携わってきた経験豊富なシスターたちと、はつらつとして瑞々しい年代のシスターたちが手を組み支え合いながら、イエスが示した福音的な生き方と多文化共同体として一つにまとまろうという修道会の志のもとに、日々奉仕と精進に励んでいます。

コニャク・ナガ族の男性に話しかける私服のMMS。
トブ村、ナガランド州、1974年。

MMS in lay dress talking to a Konyak Naga man.
Tobu village, Nagaland, 1974.

ガロの若い女性を指導するMMSと地元の保健師。
志を共にする彼女のような人々の力添えがあってこ
そ、MMSは活動を続けることができる。
ラジャバラ村、メガラヤ州、1994-1995年頃。

MMS and local health worker conduct a life-guiding
session for some Garo young women. She is our
vital partner in mission. Without such committed
people like her, we would have not been able to
carry on. Rajabala village, Meghalaya, c.1994-1995.

アッサム州でのミッションを開拓する二人のMMS。し
ばらくは仮の住まいに滞在し、足場固めに勤しんだ。
カジャルガオン、アッサム州、2005年。

Two MMS were sent to build a solid foundation of
our new mission in Assam. They stay in a temporary
house for the time being. Kajalgaon, Assam, 2005.

「シャローム」(薬物・アルコール中毒者のリハビリテーショ
ンセンター)で働くMMSとスタッフ。プログラムが完了
すると特別なお祝いをする。
チュムケディマ、ナガランド州、2006年。

MMS, one partner in mission, and two staff members in front of Shalom (a rehabilitation center for those
addicted to drugs and alcohol). The community celebrate
in a special way when a client completes the program.
Chumukedima, Nagaland, 2006.

メンディパタの生協を立ち上げたMMSとそこで働く
スタッフ。彼女は地元経済を活性化するために様々な
活動を次から次へと考え出し、行動に移している。
メンディパタ、メガラヤ州、2018年。

MMS who pioneered a Cooperative in Mendipathar
and two women working on staff. She promotes
different schemes one after another to stimulate local
economic activities. Mendipathar, Meghalaya, 2018.

# Brief history of Medical Mission Sisters in North East India

written by
Laetitia Aerthayil
edited by
Yumiko Nobue

In 1967, the Bishop of Dibrugarh Diocese requested Medical Mission Sisters (MMS) to start a small hospital in Kohima, the capital of Nagaland. Initial investigation was done and the sisters found that there was a great medical need. The "Church in India Seminar" held in 1969 in Bangalore indicated that the North East region of India (NEI) was a priority for the Church. Following this and on the basis of further investigation, MMS decided to begin a mission in Kohima among the Angami tribe. Three pioneering sisters arrived in Kohima on May 7, 1970. Their aim was to collaborate with the government in the health field. Although no government post was given to the sisters, they were provided with a facility for a dispensary, a jeep for a mobile clinic, and a yearly government grant. Mission flourished within a radius of 60 kilometers through the mobile clinic. In the course of time village health workers were trained so that they could serve their own people.

The 2nd mission was in Mendipathar, East Garo Hills (presently called North Garo Hills), Meghalaya in the diocese of Tura. A missionary priest who knew MMS in Kerala and heard about their mission in Nagaland, requested them to come to Garo Hills in order to respond to the health needs of the people. Four sisters from the South landed in Mendipathar on July 2, 1972 to work from a small clinic named St.Thomas Health Centre. It functioned three days a week. Village visits were an opening for the sisters to learn the local language, customs and traditions of the Garo tribe and to feel at home with the people. Besides the daily clinic, a few developmental projects brought increased awareness with regard to health, agriculture, and socio-economic welfare. The people were economically poor and the Mendipathar Multipurpose Cooperative Society was initiated in 1998 to support small rubber growers. It has developed greatly since then and has contributed to more economic stability for the people. Various government programs have also been accessed to help the people.

The 3rd mission begun in Rajabala village, West Garo Hills Meghalaya in the diocese of Tura on February 2, 1976. A Socio-Medical Centre became a haven for people for spiritual, physical and socio-economic aspects. The sisters responded to the needs of the people, and particularly of the children, through tuition & nutrition programs. As in Rajabala, in some of the villages, welfare programs through government subsidy and skill training were introduced. MMS trained more village health workers who are a great support in responding to the health needs of their areas. After 20 years of MMS presence in Rajabala, a parish church was established.

Three sisters were sent to Chumukedima, Nagaland in May 1993 for the 4th mission which was to collaborate with the diocese of Kohima in starting a new venture for rehabilitation of substance abusers and alcoholics. In addition, permission was given by the Bishop to begin a study house in view of promoting MMS vocations among local girls. MMS also participate in some of the parish activities, village/family visits, and non-formal education of Muslim children.

MMS mission in Assam began on February 11, 2005 in the diocese of Bongaigaon giving consideration to the needs of better communication and transportation facilities for the internal management and administration of MMS. The sisters live in the village among different ethnic groups. They are involved in the healing mission e.g. health care, empowerment of women (Self Help Groups) and children (Tuition & Nutrition), and family visits.

Today MMS continue to live healing presence among the peoples of North East India. With joy they have welcomed some women from the region into the community, and together they seek to grow more fully into life and mission according to the Gospel values and the common aspiration of MMS to become one as an inter-cultural community.

インド北東部の地図

Map of North East India

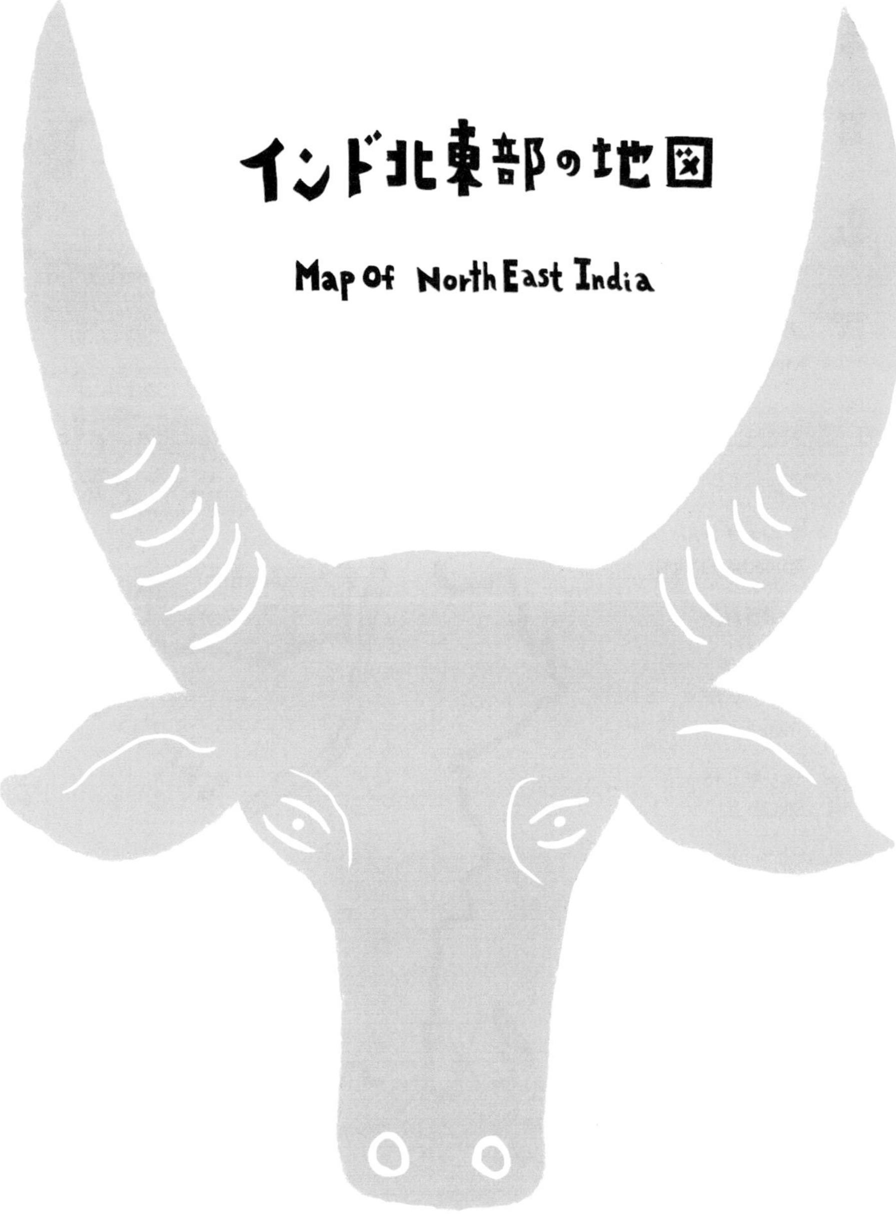

I ナガランド州
Nagaland

II マニプール州
Manipur

III アッサム州
Assam

IV メガラヤ州
Meghalaya

V アルナチャル・プラデシュ州
Arunachal Pradesh

VI ミゾラム州
Mizoram

VII トリプラ州
Tripura

VIII シッキム州
Sikkim

NEPAL

BHUTAN

ボンガイガオン
Bongaigaon

Brahmaputra River

グワハティ
Guwahati

トゥラ
Tura

IV

シロン
Shillong

BANGLADESH

VII

TIBET

ディブルガール
Dibrugarh

ディマプール
Dimapur

コヒマ
Kohima

インパール
Imphal

ナガ居住区
Naga inhabited
area

MYANMAR

凡例
———
- 地図にはインド北東部の州・地区・主要都市名、本書に登場する地名等を抜粋して掲載した。
- MMSの所在地は「M」の記号で示した。
- 縮尺はインド北東部全域および各州でそれぞれ異なる。

Explanatory notes
———
- The names written in the map include the eight states in North East India, the districts, the main cities and some places which appear in the book.
- The location of MMS convents are marked with "M".
- The size of scale is different on each of the illustrated maps.

インド北東部
North East India

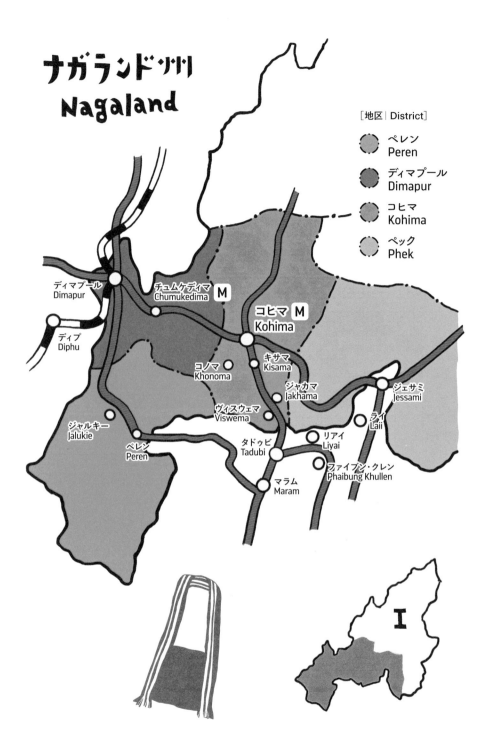

ナガランド 州
Nagaland

[地区 | District]

ペレン
Peren

ディマプール
Dimapur

コヒマ
Kohima

ペック
Phek

ディマプール
Dimapur

チュムケディマ
Chumukedima **M**

コヒマ **M**
Kohima

ディプ
Diphu

コノマ
Khonoma

キサマ
Kisama

ジャカマ
Jakhama

ジェサミ
Jessami

ヴィスウェマ
Viswema

ライ
Laii

ジャルキー
Jalukie

ペレン
Peren

タドゥビ
Tadubi

リアイ
Liyai

ファイブン・クレン
Phaibung Khullen

マラム
Maram

**I**

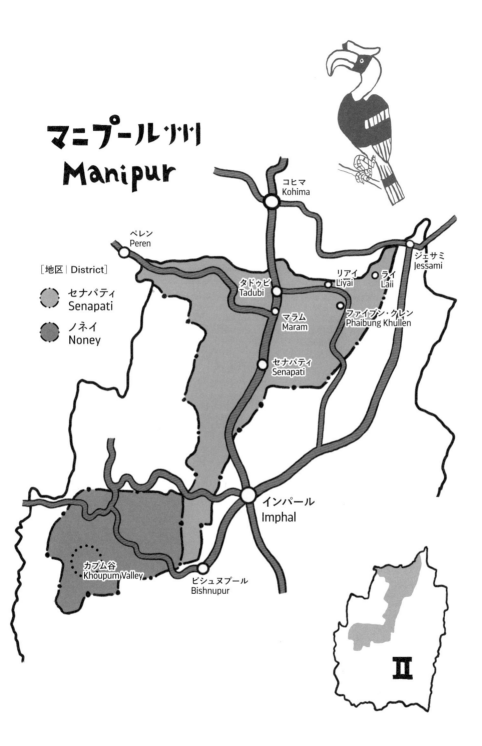

# マニプール州
# Manipur

コヒマ
Kohima

ペレン
Peren

[地区 | District]

セナパティ
Senapati

ノネイ
Noney

タドゥビ
Tadubi

リアイ
Liyai

ライ
Laii

ジェサミ
Jessami

マラム
Maram

ファイブン・クレン
Phaibung Khullen

セナパティ
Senapati

インパール
Imphal

カブム谷
Khoupum Valley

ビシュヌプール
Bishnupur

Ⅱ

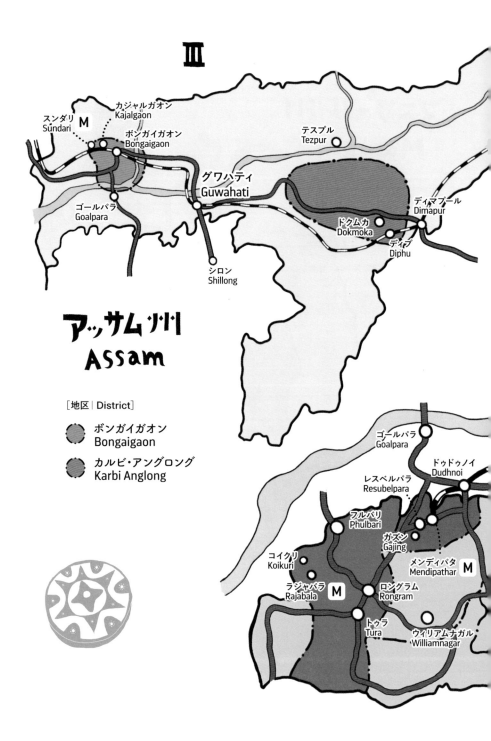

Ⅲ

カジャルガオン
Kajalgaon

スンダリ
Sundari **M**

ボンガイガオン
Bongaigaon

テスプル
Tezpur

ゴールパラ
Goalpara

グワハティ
Guwahati

ディマプール
Dimapur

ドクムカ
Dokmoka

ディプ
Diphu

シロン
Shillong

アッサム州
Assam

[地区 | District]

ボンガイガオン
Bongaigaon

カルビ・アングロング
Karbi Anglong

ゴールパラ
Goalpara

ドゥドゥノイ
Dudhnoi

レスベルパラ
Resubelpara

フルバリ
Phulbari

ガズン
Gajing

メンディパタ
Mendipathar **M**

コイクリ
Koikuri

ラジャバラ
Rajabala **M**

ロングラム
Rongram

トゥラ
Tura

ウィリアムナガル
Williamnagar

ディブルガール
Dibrugarh

# メガラヤ州

# Meghalaya

［地区｜District］

西ガロヒルズ
West Garo Hills

北ガロヒルズ
North Garo Hills

リ・ボイ
Ri Bhoi

南西カシヒルズ
South West Khasi Hills

東カシヒルズ
East Khasi Hills

西ジャンティアヒルズ
West Jaintia Hills

ジャギロード
Jagi Road

グワティ
Guwahati

ボホイレムボン
Bhoirymbong

マウブリ
Mawbri

バラパニ
Barapani

シロン
Shillong

ノングストイン
Nongstoin

ジョワイ
Jowai

マウカルワット
Mawkyrwat

チェラプンジ
Cherrapunji

ラミン
Lamin

リカイの滝
Noh Ka Likai Falls

ダウキ
Dawki

IV

凡例
——

本書には日本で一般的に知られて
いない言葉が多く登場するため、
読者にとって理解の一助となるよ
うな表現として、インド北東部に暮
らす多様な人々を示す際には適宜
「民族」や「族」などを付記してい
る。また、名称や呼称に限らず現
地で聞き書きした内容も多く含ま
れ、厳密な民族学および歴史学の
見解とは一致しない場合がある。
——

州名は一部、日英共通で
下記の省略表記とした。

ナガランド州：NL
マニプール州：MN
アッサム州：AS
メガラヤ州：ML


Explanatory notes
——

The content of this book includes
stories which the author has
seen and heard in areas of North
East India. Some of them do not
necessarily match ethnological or
historical points of view.
——

The name of the States are
sometimes written in
abbreviations as follows.

Nagaland: NL
Manipur: MN
Assam: AS
Meghalaya: ML

CHAPTER I

NAGA

山に響く民のうた

Melodies Echo in the Mountains

　　　　　　　CHAPTER I　　　NAGA

CHAPTER I    NAGA

CHAPTER I   NAGA

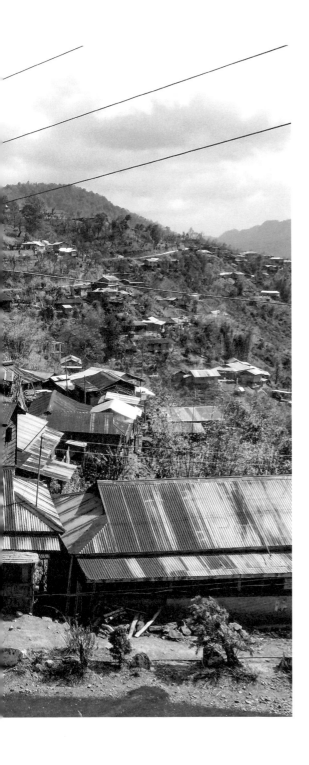

CHAPTER I     NAGA

CHAPTER I    NAGA

CHAPTER I       NAGA

CHAPTER I    NAGA

CHAPTER I    NAGA

CHAPTER I    NAGA

CHAPTER I    NAGA

# ナガの人々

そもそも「ナガ」というのは、外部の人たちが30以上のエスニックグループ（ここでは「部族」と呼ぶことにします）に属する人々につけた呼び名です。人種としてはモンゴロイドなので、顔立ちは日本人にも似ています。主にインドのナガランド州、マニプール州、アルナチャル・プラデシュ州、そしてミャンマーにまたがり、標高1,000–2,000メートルの山岳地帯に住んでいます。

彼らにはアンガミ、アオ、ロタ、マオといったそれぞれの部族としてのアイデンティティがある一方で、イギリス植民地末期以来、自分たちが同じ「ナガ民族」であるという意識が徐々に育ってきています。部族ごとに異なる母語がありますが、アッサム語とヒンズー語をミックスしたようなナガミーズ（ナガ語）と呼ばれる話し言葉があり、共通語とは言えないもののナガランド州では広く通用します。市街地になるとかなりの人が英語を話し、英語で教育する学校も目立ちます。

ナガの人々は女性も男性も実にたくましく、生命力の強さは並大抵ではありません。そして「石と土以外はなんでも食べる」と豪語するくらい、どんなものでも工夫を凝らして食べるその姿には思わず舌を巻きます。焼き畑と狩猟採集を中心に生計を立ててきた彼らは、50年ほど前まで成人男性が敵対する村を襲撃し、首を持ち帰るという首狩りの風習を残していました。19世紀になってキリスト教宣教師が入域し、現在は約9割がキリスト教徒となりましたが、それでも元来のアミニズムは彼らの生活慣習にしっかりと根付いています。今となっては日常ではほとんど用いられることがなくなりましたが、特別な行事（祭祀）には部族ごとに特色のある伝統的な多くの装飾品を身につけます。

ナガの人々は19世紀後半からイギリスとインドという大国に振り回され、太平洋戦争末期にはインパール作戦で侵攻した日本軍により多くの被害を受けました。さらに第二次世

界大戦後、ナガ民族はイギリス、インド、ミャンマーが設定した国境によって分断されてしまいました。そしてインドがイギリスから独立したその前日の1947年8月14日、ナガの人々も独立を宣言し、むごたらしい闘いが始まったのです。

この地域が2011年に至るまで許可なしでは入れなかったのも、そのような歴史背景があります。それはあまりにも複雑な事柄で、残念ながら私が正確にお伝えすることは到底できません。詳しくは、ナガランド・コヒマ生まれの作家カカ・D・イラル氏の、60年以上に及ぶナガ民族の闘争の歴史を記した本『血と涙のナガランド──語ることを許されなかった民族の物語』（木村真希子・南風島渉訳［日本語抄訳］、2011年、コモンズ）をぜひご参照ください。

ESSAY OI

## Naga people

The term Naga refers to the peoples who belong to more than 30 different ethnic groups in the states of Nagaland, Manipur, Arunachal Pradesh as well as the country of Myanmar. Their appearance is similar to Japanese people. They live mainly in the mountains, 32,000 to 65,000 feet above sea level.

Each ethnic group, such as Angami, Ao, Lotha, Mao, among others, have their own identity. Their collective identity as the Naga tribe gradually developed since towards the end of British colonization. While each tribe speaks their own language, the common language spoken among many of the tribes is Nagamese. It is a mixture of Assamese and Hindi and it is understood by most people. In the cities and towns, many people also have a good command of English and there are many English medium schools available.

The Nagas, both women and men, are strongly built and their resilience is astonishing to me. They proudly say that they eat anything except stone and soil. Indeed, they find a way to utilize whatever nature provides. Since their early days they have been making their living by slash-and-burn agriculture as well as hunting and gathering. They used to have a custom of head-hunting until almost half a century ago. In the 19th century, Christian missionaries started to come and many Nagas

コノマ村に建てられた石碑。
Stone monuments in
Khonoma village.

———

ナガはインド人ではないし、ナガの領
地はインド連邦に属するものでもな
い。我々はこの不二の真実を支持し、
いかなる犠牲を払ってでも、いつの
時でも守り抜くのである。
ナガランド連邦政府初代大統領
クリャサニサ・セイエ
1956年7月12日-1959年2月18日

Nagas are not Indians; their territory
is not a part of the Indian Union.
We shall uphold and defend this
unique truth at all costs and always.
Khriesaneisa Seyie, First President,
Federal Government of Nagaland,
12th July 1956 to 18th February 1959

1995年にコノマ村に建てられた
この石碑には、1947年8月14日に
掲揚されたナガランドの旗の図柄
の下に、以下の言葉とともに男女
46名の名前が刻まれている。
The design on the top of the
monument in Khonoma village,
erected in 1995, is based on the
flag hoisted on August 14, 1947.

———

コノマ村の人々は、自由なナガ民族
の国家という理念のために命を捧げ
た。我々は彼らのことを敬意を持って
記憶にとどめ、その志を守り続ける。
1956-1992

These men and women of Khonoma
gave their lives for the vision of a free
Naga nation. We remember and
salute them and still hold fast to their
vision. 1956-1992

were converted. Alongside Christian beliefs, the spirit of Animism is still strongly prevalent in their day to day life. During traditional festivals and rituals, people have unique attire with ornaments and accessories, nowadays used only for special occasions.

Since the 19th century, the Naga people have suffered from political violence, under both the British and Indian authorities. Towards the end of World War II (WWII), the Japanese army invaded towards Imphal and turned their land, especially Kohima, into a fierce battlefield. Furthermore, the people were divided by the national borders set between India and Myanmar after WWII. India gained its independence from the British on the 15th of August 1947. Just a day before that, the Naga had also declared their independence. However, it was not recognized internationally and their harsh struggle for freedom has ensued for decades.

Until 2011, no visitors, neither Indian nationals nor foreigners were allowed to enter the area without a permit. To learn more of the complicated and sensitive history and the incredible stories of the Naga people, I recommend the book *Nagaland and India: The Blood and the Tears* (Kaka. D. Iralu, 2000).

# 第二次世界大戦──ナガと日本兵

ナガランド州の州都コヒマ。ここに来た人が必ず訪れるのが、第二次世界大戦で戦死した英連邦軍兵士たちの墓地です。記録によると、英印軍は17,587人が犠牲になりました[01]。墓地全体を見渡せるほど小高くなったところには十字架があり、その下の石碑にはこう記されています。「ここに眠る同志はコヒマ戦においてインドを侵攻せんとする日本軍と戦い、1944年4月についにそれを撃退したのであった」。コヒマは日本軍と英連邦軍の激戦地だったのです。整然と並ぶ無数の墓石にはイギリス兵と北東部出身を含むインド兵とネパール兵の名が刻まれていますが、日本兵のものはなく、彼らの遺骨のほとんどはまだ山の奥深くに残されたままです。

日本軍は太平洋戦争で占領したビルマ（現ミャンマー）を経由し、そこからインパールを攻めるべくさらに西へ進んでいきました。あまりに無謀だったと悪名高いインパール作戦。その結果、この地域一帯で3万人以上の日本兵が犠牲となりました。彼らはこの奥深いジャングルで、食べ物も水もなく、大雨に打たれ、激しい下痢、蚊の猛襲、いつ襲いかかってくるかもしれない獣と死の恐怖に苦しみながら母や恋人のことを想い、ついには命を落としていったのです。ほとんどが十代後半か二十歳そこそこの若者でした。

当時の戦いを現地の人々は「ジャパン・ウォー（日本戦争）」と記憶しており、行く先々で私が日本人と知ると、日本兵たちのことをいろいろ聞かせてくれました。お祖父さまから教わったと、「白地に赤く」で始まる日本の軍歌を歌ってくれたことも一度ならずありました。

私たちがよく訪問するマニプール州のカプム谷では、そこに住むロンマイ・ナガ族の人が「日本兵は勤勉で、優秀で、真面目だったそうです。僕らにとって、それが日本人のイメージです」と穏やかな口調で話してくれました。またある時、ディマプールで会ったポチュリ・ナガ族の人は、初対面の私に言

いました。「当時、僕の村の人たちはイギリス兵から『日本は敵だ』と散々聞かされていた。日本兵が襲撃してきた時には、僕たちは首狩り族だったからその兵隊さんの首をとった。そして記念として、その日に生まれた赤ん坊にジャパネという名前をつけたんだよ」。

私はこの地でインパール作戦のことを知って以来、ナガランドとマニプールを車やバスで行き来するたびに、窓の外を眺めながらかつての日本兵たちに思いを巡らせるようになりました。社会人類学者である中根千枝氏は1954年にインド北東部を訪れた際、コヒマにある「草ぼうぼうのジャングル」となっていた日本兵の墓地に案内された時のことを以下のように記録しています。イギリス兵の遺体は集められ政府が作った立派な墓地に安置されたのに、日本兵はジャングルの中に放置されたまま。それではあまりに気の毒だと、ナガの人々がはっきり日本兵とわかる亡骸を集めて埋葬したその場所には「ちょうど人間のからだくらいの大きさの土まんじゅう」が「少くとも五、六百体はありそうだった」[02]。

また最近になっては、コヒマやインパールといった地名は戦いの舞台としてのみ語られ、現地の人々がどれほどの被害を受けたのかもいまだよくわかっていないということを知る機会がありました。今まで聞かれることのなかった声を集め、彼らの視点から見直すことによってこそこの戦いの実態が明らかになるのではないか、と日本の研究者も現地調査に取り組んでいるそうです[03]。

多くの犠牲者の安らかな眠りを祈りつつ、同じ過ちを私たちは決して繰り返してはいけないと思わずにはいられません。

# World War II: The Naga people and Japan

Any visitor to Kohima would not fail to go to the War Cemetery where soldiers of the British Allied Forces during World War II (WWII) are buried. According to the record, the numbers of the casualties of British and Indian are about 18,000.[01] Under a big white cross erected on the elevated terrace of the cemetery, there is a stone monument on which is marked: "Here around the tennis court of the deputy commissioner lie men who fought in the battle of Kohima in which they and their comrades finally halted the invasion of India by the forces of Japan in April 1944." Numerous gravestones in the cemetery are of British and Indian including Naga soldiers while the remains of the Japanese are still left out somewhere deep in the mountains of Nagaland, Manipur and Myanmar.

During WWII, the Japanese army invaded Burma (present day Myanmar), and proceeded further from there, towards the west to attack Imphal. Called the Imphal Operation, it is notorious for its reckless strategy and disastrous casualties. More than 30,000 Japanese soldiers died in the offensive mainly due to starvation, extreme fatigue and diseases such as diarrhea and malaria. It was hell in thick jungles, no food, no water, torrential rains, fierce mosquito attacks, wild animals and facing certain death. In the midst of all that, many young soldiers lost their precious lives for nothing.

People in the area remember the battle as "The Japan War." Once they found out that I am Japanese, they proceeded to tell me stories of Japanese soldiers. More than once, I heard one particular Japanese military song which they say they learned from their grandfathers.

Until I came to Kohima, I have to confess with shame that I was ignorant about the Imphal Operation. Dr. Chie Nakane, a well known Japanese social anthropologist, went to North East India in 1954 and recorded her visit to a jungle-like "graveyard" for the Japanese soldiers in Kohima. While the bodies of the allies were collected and put in a grand graveyard prepared by the government, the Japanese were simply left in the forest to rot. The Naga felt such a pity for them that they gathered the bodies of Japanese soldiers and buried them in a corner of Kohima. There were several hundred burial mounds just about the size of a human body.[02] Later in Japan, I had a chance to participate in an online seminar and realized that nothing much is revealed yet as to the damage to the local people.[03] As I learn more about its history, I find myself pondering the many victims, including the local people, whenever I travel along the mountainous roads in Nagaland and Manipur.

I cannot help but pray for the souls of all the lives that were lost and I am convinced that we must never repeat the same mistake ever again.

01  S. Woodburn Kirby, *The War Against Japan, Vol. III: The Decisive Battles* (HMSO, 1962).

02  中根千枝『未開の顔・文明の顔』中央公論新社、1990年、p. 69–70。
Chie Nakane, *Mikai no Kao, Bunmei no Kao* [ Faces of the uncivilized, faces of civilization ], Chuokoron-shinsha, 1990, p. 69–70.

03  「インパール作戦 現地被害・記憶・和解」(オンラインセミナー)、明治学院大学国際平和研究所、2021年2月22日。
"Attack Imphal: Local damage, memory, reconciliation (Online Seminar)", International Peace Research Institute Meiji Gakuin University, 22 February 2021.

コヒマの扶助者聖母・カテドラル教会にある記念碑。1989年にコヒマ戦生存者と戦没者遺族から平和と感謝の祈りを込めて教会建立の寄付がなされたことが記してある。

On the grounds of the Cathedral of Mary Help of Christians in Kohima, there is a memorial plaque, given in 1989, by WWII survivors of the Japanese army and the bereaved families of the Japanese soldiers. The words express deep gratitude to the people in Nagaland for their prayers for the souls of the victims of WWII, and offers their sincere prayers for world peace.

CHAPTER I    NAGA

CHAPTER I    NAGA

CHAPTER I NAGA

CHAPTER I          NAGA

CHAPTER I  NAGA

CHAPTER I　　N A G A

P. 034–035
セナパティ
Senapati, MN

コヒマからインパールに向かう国道からの眺め。ナガ民族は伝統的に焼き畑で耕作しているが、棚田栽培も次第に広まってきた。あちこちに美しい棚田があり、目を奪われる。

A view from National Highway between Kohima and Imphal. While slash-and-burn is done traditionally, terrace cultivation has become popular where it is possible and its landscape is eye catching.

P. 036
ライ村
Laii village, MN

冬はかなり冷え込む。私が最初に訪れたのは1月。持ってきたものをすべて着込み、もらった毛布を全部かけてもとにかく寒くて眠れなかった。

It is rather cold in winter in Laii village. I visited there in January. It was too cold to sleep even though I put on all the clothes I had and all the blankets offered during the night.

P. 037
コノマ村
Khonoma village, NL

山あいに広がる見事な棚田があるコノマは歴史的な村だ。イギリス植民地時代には35年に及ぶ熾烈な反英闘争を展開した。また、インドがイギリスから独立してから初期のナガ民族運動を指導した「民族運動の父」とも呼ばれるA. Z. ピゾの出身地でもある。村のあちこちに戦闘で命を落とした人々の名前が刻まれた石碑がある。

Magnificent terraced rice field in Khonoma village. The village is a historical place as people fought against the British for 35 years under their rule. Also, it is a birthplace of A. Z. Phizo, the Father of the Nation. There are many stone monuments throughout the village to commemorate the freedom fighters.

P. 038
コノマ村
Khonoma village, NL

コノマ村にあるダフという集会場所。ナガの人々の間では物事はすべて話し合いによって決められた。

The meeting place called *Dahou* in the village. All the decisions were made after discussion among themselves in Naga culture.

P. 039
コノマ村
Khonoma village, NL

村のカトリック教会。

Catholic church in the village.

P. 040–041
ペック
Phek, NL

ナガの人々は外部からの侵入を防ぐために、丘の上や山の頂に村を拓いたという。

Naga people used to set up their village on the top of a mountain or hill in order to protect themselves from the invasion by outsiders.

P. 042
チュマケディマ
Chumukedima, NL

ディマプールとコヒマをつなぐ国道にある大きな門。図柄はミトゥン（牛）とホーンビル（鳥）の頭。コヒマに入るための許可書が必要だった頃には、ここに検問所があった。

The gate on the highway between Dimapur and Kohima. The designs are the head of Mithun and Hornbill. There used to be a check point when a permit was necessary to visit Kohima.

..................................

..................................

プナナマイ
Punanamei, MN

カトリック教会にある記念碑。ミトゥンはナガランド固有種の
牛で、その肉は体に良い上に美味。太い角は角笛や祭礼用の
ジョッキなどにも使われる。ミトゥンの頭の絵はこのようにシンボ
ルとして、いろいろなところで目にする。

Monument in a Catholic church. *Mithun* is a cow, an endemic
species of Nagaland. According to my Naga friend, they
consider it "Nagaland National Animal." Its fat big horn is
used for a musical horn or a mug for a festive occasion. I have
seen the symbol of the head of *Mithun* in different places in
Nagaland.

P. 045
ファイブン・クレン村
Phaibung Khullen village, MN
ナガの伝統的な家。入り口の屋根の上に木製の大きな角（キケ、チカ、カイチャイなど部族によって名前が異なる）が掲げてある。これは雄鶏の頭のシンボルとも牛の頭を象ったものとも言われる。この装飾は、男性が結婚しその伴侶の女性と共に村人すべてを最高の食事でもてなすことのできた家だけが許される特権で、富を持つ人でなければできない。それが果たされた暁には二つの石を曳いてきてそれを建てる儀式が遂行される。

A traditional house of Naga people. The wooden horn at the top of the roof has a different name such as *kikie*, *chika*, *kai chei* or other, according to the tribes. It is said to be a symbol of a cock's head or buffalo's horn. To be able to erect such a wooden horn, the man along with his wife must attain the highest level of generosity by giving very fine free meals to others. To solemnize the achievement, a pulling of stone ceremony is held in which two stones are erected. The event is called Feast of Merit.

P. 046–047
ヴィスウェマ村
Viswema village, NL
ヴィスウェマ村からの眺め。年に一度、村の人々はこの山に登り、わらを集めてほうきを作る。そしてそのほうきに乗って、山から滑り下りるという風習があるらしい。

A view from Viswema village. Once a year, the villagers climb the mountain to make brooms, and slide down with them, holding the handle part.

........................................

P. 048
カプム谷
Khoupum Valley, MN
日曜日のミサへ行く村人。女性が手に持つのは奉納するウリ。

Villagers on the way to Sunday Mass. What she carries is a big squash as an offering.

P. 049
ファイブン・クレン村
Phaibung Khullen village, MN
畑仕事に向かうプーマイ・ナガ族の人々。

Poumai Naga people going to the fields.

........................................

P. 050–053
カプム谷
Khoupum Valley, MN

ディマプールからチュムケディマに向かう道は大々的な道路拡張工事の真っ最中で、ひどい状況だ。そこへ乗合オートの乗り心地最低最悪である最後部座席に座ったものだからたまったものではない。必死に手すりにしがみつきひたすら耐える私を横に、途中から乗ってきたナガのおばさんは車体がジャンプするたびに「アバババ！」と叫び、少し落ち着いたと思ったらお隣さんとおしゃべりを始め、今度は「ガハハハ！」と大笑い。なんたるタフネス！まったく恐れ入りました。

The main road between Dimapur and Chumukedima is under major construction. Naga roads are notorious for their condition to begin with, and now the situation is truly horrendous. Once, I took a shared auto from the Dimapur train station to Chumukedima, sitting on the back seat, which was a big mistake. All I could do was cling to the handrail with my mouth tightly shut. Two Naga ladies got in and sat next to me. Well, they screamed each time the auto jumped up, and as soon as the road became a bit smoother, they started to chat along roaring with loud laughter. What toughness!

ここから少し離れたところに、日本兵が隠れていたという大きな岩があると村人が教えてくれた。

Villagers told me that there is a huge rock not far from there where some Japanese soldiers used to hide during WWII.

. . . . . . . . . . . . . . . . . . . . . . . . . . . . . .

P. 054
タドゥビ
Tadubi, MN

キャベツを道沿いで売るプーマイ・ナガ族の女性。ここでは「ジャパニーズ・キャベツ」と呼ばれる特産品のキャベツをあたり一面に栽培している。

Poumai Naga woman selling cabbage on the roadside. A particular kind of cabbage called "Japanese cabbage" by local people are cultivated popularly in the area.

. . . . . . . . . . . . . . . . . . . . . . . . . . . . . .

P. 054
カプム谷
Khoupum Valley, MN

朝食をよそう寄宿舎のロンマイ・ナガ族の中学生。生徒たちは朝5時には起床し、自分たちで朝食を準備する。主食のお米をしっかり食べて長い一日に備える。

Ruangmei Naga students in boarding house serving breakfast. They get up at 5am and prepare breakfast by themselves. Their stable food is rice.

ディマプールとコヒマを結ぶ国道
National highway between Dimapur and Kohima, NL

コヒマは山の頂上にあるが、数年前から山を大々的に切り崩して4車線の国道を建設中。完成すれば、アッサム州へのアクセスが俄然良くなる。曲がりくねった道は軍隊の車両、大型バスやトラックが走り抜けるたびに、ものすごい量の埃が舞いあがる。大雨が降ったり、山を爆破することで引き起こされる土砂崩れで通行止めになることも日常茶飯事。数時間足止めを食らうことも珍しくない。

A major construction on the highway between Kohima and Assam is going on. It will be four lanes and the transport convenience will be so much faster and easier once it is completed. Whenever buses and trucks as well as military vehicles pass by on the winding road, tremendous amounts of dust are whirled up. Landslides due to heavy rain and explosion to break mountains are daily events as well. It is not unusual to be held back on the road for hours.

P. 055
リアイ村
Liyai village, MN

水汲みに行くナガの少年たち。籠の中に水瓶が入っている。

Naga boys on their way to fetch water. Each carries a water pot in the basket.

P. 056
リアイ村
Liyai village, MN

孫を抱くプーマイ・ナガ族の女性。

Poumai Naga woman with her grandchild.

P. 057
ルソマ村
Riisoma village, NL
ナガの少年たち。
Naga boys.

P. 058
コヒマ
Kohima, NL
ナガ独特のライスビールを作る
アンガミ・ナガ族の女性。発芽

した餅米で発酵させた発泡性
のお酒で、濁り酒のように見え
る。アルコール度数は低いとい
うが、私は少し口にしただけで
顔が赤くなった気がした。
Angami Naga woman
making Naga rice beer.
They say its alcohol content
is minimum, but I found my
face getting red only with a
few sips.

P. 058
ジャカマ村
Jakhama village, NL

一本の木から作られたクピとい
うお皿から食べるアンガミ・ナ
ガ族の女性。
Angami Naga woman with
a traditional wooden dish
called *Khouphi*.

P. 059
ヴィスウェマ村
Viswema village, NL
昔ながらのナガの家には土間
がある。ここで料理し、食事を
し、子どもたちは宿題をし、家
族が団欒する。

タドゥビ
Tadubi, MN
私に同伴していた神父さんにおすそ分けをしたいと、収穫した
キャベツを籠から取り出すプーマイ・ナガ族の姉妹。
Poumai Naga sisters want to share their cabbage with a
priest whom I was traveling with.

There is always an earthen floor in a traditional Naga house. It is a common space for family. They cook, eat, study and just spend a good time together.

..................................

P. 060–061
ヴィスウェマ村
Viswema village, NL
登校前に従姉妹に髪を結ってもらうアンガミ・ナガ族の少女。

Angami Naga girl having her hair tied by her cousin before she goes to school.

..................................

P. 062
リアイ村
Liyai village, MN

ダオという鉈。用途によって、違うダオを使い分ける。山で木を切る時はもちろん、台所でも包丁として必ず置いてある。かつては戦闘にも使われた。私の友人は亡き父上のダオを大事にとってあるそうだ。

Traditional Naga knives, called *Dao*. Different *Dao* are used according to different purposes – kitchen knife, axe, weapon... My friend told me that she keeps the *Dao* of her late father as a precious thing.

..................................

P. 062
リアイ村
Liyai village, MN
ナガの男性はダオを腰につけたジエサという入れ物に収めて持ち運ぶ。

*Dao* in *Ziesa* at the back of a Naga man's waist.

P. 063
ルソマ村
Riisoma village, NL
伝統的な焼き畑で歌をうたいながら働くアンガミ・ナガ族の女性たち。

Angami Naga women working in the slash-and-burn field, singing a song.

P. 064–066
カブム谷
Khoupum Valley, MN
家で機織りをするナガの女性。

Naga woman weaving in their house.

P. 066–067

コヒマ
Kohima, NL

デザインはそれぞれの部族で
異なる。
Its design is unique to each
ethnic group.

P. 068–070

ナガランド州、マニプール州
NL, MN

ナガの人々。90歳を超えても
若々しくまだまだ元気な人に出
会うことは珍しくなかった。
I often came across Naga
elders who remain very
strong physically into their
90's.

これはナガの知人から聞いたこと。「時は第一次世界大戦、イ
ンドはイギリス領。イギリスとフランスは連合軍としての同志
だった。2,000人近くのナガがイギリスの命令で労働者としてフ
ランスに連れられていった。まずムンバイまでは列車、そこから
は船だ。兵役後、全員が無事に帰国できたわけではない。が、
帰国したナガたちはフランスで見聞きした革命のことを仲間に
も伝えた。いつかは自分たちも、と刺激されたのだ」。もともと
独立心の強い民族だ。その彼らが革命のうねりを目の当たりに
したのだった。第一次大戦も第二次大戦もナガの人々にどれほ
ど大きな影響をもたらしたことか、と考えると感慨深い。

A Naga friend of mine told me once: During WWI,
India was ruled by the British. By their order, about 2,000
Naga people were taken to France as coolies (laborers)
because England and France were allies. They went by
train up to Mumbai, then by boat to France. Not all managed to come back to Nagaland after their service.
However, those who returned home shared with their fellow men about the revolutionary movement that they saw
among the French and it inspired their own dream of
achieving the same victory one day.

P. 071

ヴィスウェマ村
Viswema village, NL

アンガミ・ナガ族の姉妹。朝か
ら食欲旺盛だ。
Angami Naga sisters enjoy-
ing their hearty breakfast.

P. 071

コノマ村
Khonoma village, NL

荷物の入った籠を担ぐアンガ
ミ・ナガ族の女性たち。
Angami Naga women, each
carrying a basket of goods.

P. 072

カプム谷
Khoupum Valley, MN

息子の体を洗うロンマイ・ナガ
族の女性。男の子の背中には
蒙古斑がある。
Ruangmei Naga woman
bathing her son who still
has a Mongolian spot.

P. 081

コヒマ
Kohima, NL

コヒマ戦没者墓地。無数の墓
が整然と並んでいる。

The Kohima War Cemetery. Orderly rows of numerous graves fill the grounds.

p. 082–083
コヒマ
Kohima, NL

上から、アンガミ・ナガ兵の墓石、イギリス兵の墓石、インド兵の墓石（文字はウルドゥー語）。

From the top, Tombstone of an Angami Naga soldier, Tombstone of a British soldier, Tombstone of an Indian soldier (script is Urdu).

p. 084–085
コヒマ
Kohima, NL

コヒマの街。コヒマの雰囲気はどこか変わったように思う。そういえば初めて訪れた時、知人が「コヒマからディマプールに来ると、"インドに戻ってきた"って気がする」と言っていたのはこういうことか、と納得したものだ。2011年からは特別な許可がなくても入れるようになり外からの訪問者が増えたこともあってか、かつてほど強烈に「ここはインドではない…」と感じることはなくなった。

The town of Kohima. When I visited Kohima for the first time in 2005, it

コヒマ
Kohima, NL

放棄されたイギリス軍の戦車。戦車の横に石碑があり、こう記されている。「1944年5月6日、モンスーンによる大雨で危険な状況の中、このイギリス軍戦車は日本軍の攻撃にあったが、中の兵士たちはなんとか無事に脱出した。ここで戦ったすべての兵士の勇敢な行動と犠牲を記念するために、この戦車はそのままの状態で残しておくことになった」。

There is a stone monument next to the tank which says: On May 6, 1944, this tank was attacked by the Japanese army in the torrential rain, but the soldiers inside managed to escape. It was decided to leave it here to commemorate the bravery and sacrifice of all the soldiers who fought in the battle.

was very different from the parts of India I had come to know. I understood what one of my acquaintances meant when he had said earlier: "It feels as if I arrive back in India when I reach Dimapur from Kohima." It has changed much over the years. Since 2011 a permit is no longer required to visit and there are more outsiders coming in. It used to surprise me how different Kohima was from the rest of India. I don't experience it like that any more.

p. 086

ジャカマ村
Jakhama village, NL

日本軍によって建てられた最初の学校の跡地にある石碑。村の人々は日本語を教わり、時には負傷した日本兵の治療もしたという。この石碑を見せてくれた村人の叔父さまは、色白で大きな体格をしていたからかイギリス兵と間違われて日本兵に射殺されてしまったのだが、日本人である私に気持ちよく接してくれた。また彼のお祖父さまは第二次世界大戦の時にナガ民族評議会（NNC）の会長で、ナガ独立運動で重要人物だったとのこと。英語が話せて通訳もでき、日本兵に気に入られ日本に来るように散々誘われたが、奥さまが断固として反対したそうだ。

The monument at the site of the first Japanese school built by the Japanese army in Jakhama village. I was fortunate to come, by chance, across a person from this village. He shared with me a few stories: He told me that the villagers took care of the Japanese soldiers who were injured in battle. The man's uncle, being fair and largely built, was mistaken for a British and shot dead by a Japanese soldier. His grandfather was the President of the Naga National Council. Grandfather had a good command of English and did some translations for the Japanese soldiers. They appreciated him so much that they repeatedly asked him to come to Japan, but his wife never allowed him.

p. 087

ライ村
Laii village, MN

山を背景に立つプーマイ・ナガ族の高校生。

Poumai Naga students in Laii village. The Japanese military aircraft was found in the jungle behind them.

p. 088–089

ライ村
Laii village, MN

この村からほど近い山の中にイギリス軍に撃墜された日本の軍機が墜落した。その後、誰にも気がつかれずに白骨化した遺体が発見されたのだと聞いた。話によると、「生き残った一人はテントを建ててしばらく生き延びていたようだが、誰も助けに来なくてやがてそのまま死んだらしい」。

A villager told me: At the time of Japan War, a Japanese military aircraft was shot down by the British into a deep mountain behind the village. Nobody knew until some villagers found skeletons much later.

p. 090–091

コヒマ
Kohima, NL

王たるキリスト教会。この教会の大多数はアンガミ・ナガ族。日曜日のミサには部族特有のショールを纏う。

Christ the King Parish. The majority of the parishioners belong to Angami Naga tribe. Both women and men put on their traditional shawl to attend the Sunday Mass.

p. 092–093

チュムケディマ
Chumukedima, NL

コヒマ
Kohima, NL

ナガの人々にとって歌は生活そのものだという。コヒマで田植えの歌の練習を見せてもらう機会があった。9人のメンバーが3つのパートに分かれ、お互いの声に注意深く耳を傾けながら音程を確認する。楽譜はない。その後、タティという一弦楽器と共に力強くもどこか物哀しいハーモニーを作りあげていった。

They say that songs are an integral part of life for the Naga people. I had an opportunity to observe their singing practice after Sunday Mass. There is no musical score. Listening to each other, they create a powerful and yet somewhat melancholic harmony with a single stringed instrument called Tati.

---

ミサの始まりにある行列を先導するアディバシの女性たちと初聖体を授かる子どもたち。この教会にはナガ民族をはじめ様々なエスニックグループが所属しているが、カトリック信徒として初めてキリストの体であるパンをいただく初聖体は、教会こぞってお祝いする。ディマプールにあるナガランド州で初めてのカトリック共同体は、20世紀初頭、主に現在のジャーカンド州から茶園と鉄道建設の労働者としてやってきたアディ

バシの人々だ。彼らが住んでいるところは駅からさほど遠くないのに、カエルの鳴き声が響く田園が広がり大層穏やかである。そこはなぜか時間の流れが違うように感じられた。

The Adivasi women lead the procession and the children who are to receive their first communion. There are several ethnic groups which belong to the parish, and the whole parish community celebrate together special occasions such as the First

Communion. In Dimapur, there is the first Catholic Community of NL which consist of Adivasi people.

.............

P. 094-095
チュムケディマ
Chumukedima, NL

初聖体のミサ後。緊張がほどけ、和んだ雰囲気に包まれ

た。これからお祝いのイベントが催される近くの学校まで行進する。

After the liturgy of First Communion. The atmosphere is now relaxed. They are about to go to another place for the celebration.

........................

P. 096
コヒマ
Kohima, NL
カトリック信者の慣例である十字を切るために、ミサが始まる前に手を聖水（司祭によって祝別された水）に浸すアンガミ・ナガ族の女性。聖堂の入り口には聖水が入った聖水盤が置かれている。

Angami Naga woman dipping her finger into Holy Water and make a sign of the cross before Mass, which is a common practice of a Catholic.

........................

P. 097
コヒマ
Kohima, NL
正装した教会の女性コーラス部。纏っているのはアンガミ・ナガ族のショールと腰巻き。インド北東部の女性たちは「おそろい」を着るのが好きなのかもしれない。

The women's church choir in formal dress. It seems people in North East India in general like to put on the same dress for a formal occasion.

........................

P. 097
チュムケディマ
Chumukedima, NL
ブラスバンド部の高校生。初聖体のミサ後の行進は彼女たちが先頭を行った。

High School Brass-band students. They led the procession to the venue for the parish celebration after the first communion Mass.

........................

P. 098-099
キサマ村
Kisama village, NL
アンガミ・ナガ族が毎年2月に行うセクレニー（地元ではプーサニーとして知られる）という浄めの祭りの大事な一部であるテクラ・ヒエの様子。同じ年代の男女のグループが3日間こうして座り続け、伝統の歌を一日中うたい続ける。人々はお供え物を持ってきて聴き入るそうだ。

The scene of *Thekra Hie*, a part of the *Sekrenyi*, which is the Angami Naga's annual festival of purification in February.

P. 100-103
キサマ村
Kisama village, NL
上から、コニャク・ナガ族、セマ・ナガ族、アオ・ナガ族、ゼリアング・ナガ族、キャムンガン・ナガ族、ポチュリ・ナガ族。

From the top, Konyak Naga, Sema Naga, Ao Naga, Zeliang Naga, Khiamniungan Naga, Pochury Naga.

........................

P. 104
ザパミ村
Zapami village, NL
山で集めた薪を担いで家路につくナガの女性。

Naga woman going home with a load of fire wood collected in the woods.

ナガ民族には一年を通して部族ごとにお祭りがある。それに加
えて、毎年12月の第1週にはナガランド州政府による「ホーンビ
ル・フェスティバル」がキサマ村で催される。華やかな期間中に
はそれぞれの部族がダイナミックな儀式や踊りを歌と共に披露
したり、伝統的な食事を試すことができたりと、国内外から多
くの観光客が訪れる。ホーンビルは鳥の名前（和名サイチョウ）。
白に黒い線が入ったその羽は、頭飾りなどによく使われる。

Naga people have their own festivals according to their
tribes and villages throughout the year. Besides these,
there is an annual grand festival once a year organized by
the State of Nagaland for the whole Naga communities.
Lots of tourists both Indians and foreigners come to
enjoy. Hornbill is the name of a bird whose feather is
commonly used as a decoration of the hat.

# 石

石はナガ民族にとって、村の出来事や先祖たちのことを口承する道具でもあったようです。道沿いや村の中に建立された石のそばに村人が集まり、それにまつわる逸話を語り合いました[01]。

ナガランド州の州都コヒマからマニプール州に入ったところを東に向かうと、ナガ民族に属する部族のマオ族とプーマイ族の村々があります。その一つ、トブマイ村に差し掛かると大きな石があり、その横に小さな石碑が建っています。石碑には、「これは不思議な魔力を持つ石です。この上で刈り取った籠一つ分の稲を乾かすと倍になりました。そのおかげでトブマイ村の先祖たちは豊かになって、旅人に食べ物や飲み物を提供したものです」と書かれています。

トブマイ村にある大きな石。ここの木陰で一休みしようとしていた二人の女性が下ろした籠を見ると、どちらも籠いっぱいに青々とした野菜が入っていた。ほどなくして、制服を着た小学1年生くらいの少女が、小さなバケツいっぱいのじゃがいもを持ってやってきた。

A big stone in Tobumai village. When we reached the stone, two women arrived to take a break. Both carried a basket full of fresh green vegetables. Soon after, a girl in school uniform that looked to be in first grade came with a small bucket full of potatoes.

同行していたプーマイ族の神父さんが、さらに付け加えて言いました。「籠一つ分が籠二つ分になるというのだから、当然のことながら村人は誰でもここで稲を乾かしたいと思っていた。ある時、二人の女性がかち合い、喧嘩になった。結局勝ったほうが乾かしたんだが、負けたほうが後になってその腹いせに腰巻きでその石を叩き、さらに石の上でゴマを焼いた。悲しいかなそれ以来、石は魔力を失ってしまったのさ」。

石にまつわるこんな奇談も聞きました。ナガ民族には「回り合せの石」という石があり、それを手にすると所有欲をコントロールできなくなる盗癖に取り憑かれ、そして最後には自分の命を失うことになる、というのです。それは稀にではあるけれど、ほんとうに起こるということでした。ちょっと気味の悪いお話です。

## Stone

For the people of Naga, stones are one of the tools of their oral traditions. They gather around stones along the country roads or in villages and enjoy telling and listening to different stories.[01]

In the North Eastern part of Manipur state, there are two tribal factions, the Mao and the Poumai, who are categorized as Nagas. On a bright sunny day in summer, I took a trip with local people to visit some of these villages. Just before entering Tobumai village, there was a big stone and a small stone monument which said the following: "This is a mega-lithic fetish stone. If a basketful of paddies was scorched on this stone, it would be able to collect double the amount. This stone made the Tobumai forefathers so rich that they provided food and drinks to the travelers."

A Poumai priest who was guiding us added to the story: "Well, one basket of paddies becomes two! Of course, all the villagers wanted to dry their paddies on this stone. One day, two women reached the stone at the same time. They fought over who would dry their paddy first. The loser felt so upset

that she hit the stone bitterly with her loincloth and then burned sesame seeds on it. Alas! The stone lost its power and did not make the paddies double any longer."
I heard another strange story. It is called, "luck stone." Once you hold onto it, your desire to possess things becomes out of control and you will be addicted to stealing till you lose your own life. It is extremely rare, but they say such a thing does happen. What a spooky stone...

01  森田勇造『写真で見るアジアの少数民族3 南アジア編』三和書籍、2012年、p.10。
Yuzo Morita, *Shashin de Miru Ajia no Shosuminzoku 3: Minami Ajia hen*［Asian Ethnic Minorities in Photographs 3: South Asia section］, Sanwa-shoseki, 2012, p.10.

ファイブン・クレン村の入り口にある岩ほどに大きな無数の石。村の誰かの命日など特別な日のために山から運んできたもので、村人たちは一つ一つの石に魂が宿っていると信じている。

You are welcomed by countless huge stones as you enter the village of Phaibung Khullen. Villagers bring them from the mountains to commemorate special occasions such as significant death anniversaries of villagers. They believe a spirit lives in each stone.

ロンマイ・ナガ族の伝統衣装
Ruangmei Naga girls in their traditional dress

ガロ族の伝統衣装
Garo young men and women
in their cultural dress

**セマ・ナガ族の晴れ着**
Sema Naga girls dressed up in their Sunday best

COLUMN 01          DRESS

ラバ族の伝統衣装
Rabha young man and woman
in their traditional dress

ハジョン族の普段着
Hajong woman in her ordinary dress

ラバ族の普段着
Garo young women in
Rabha's ordinary dress

カルビ族の伝統衣装はピニ（ショール）、ペコック（腰巻き）、ワム・コック（ベルト）の３点セットになっている。
Karbi's traditional dress has three parts: *Pini* (shawl), *Pekok* (loincloth), and *Vam-Kok* (belt).

アッサム人のムガ・サリー。素材はムガ・シルクという特別な絹。
Assamese woman in Muga saree made of Muga silk, a specialty of Assam.

サンタリ族のパンチダシというサリー。
左の女性が正装。

Santhali women in *Panchidasi*. The woman
on the left is in a formal outfit.

ボド族のドコナという普段着。ドコナの
上にファスラというショールを纏う。

Bodo school teachers in their ordinary
dress of Bodo called *Dokhona* with a
shawl called *Fasra*.

アッサム人の伝統衣装はサドル（ブラウス）、
メッケラ（腰巻き）、ガムサ（小さなショール）
の3点セット。ビフという民族舞踊を踊る
時にもこれを着る。

Assamese women in their traditional dress,
which has three parts: *Sador* (blouse),
*Mekhela* (loincloth), and *Gamosa* (small shawl).
They wear it when they dance their folk
dance called *Bihu*.

アンガミ・ナガ族（左）と
イムチェンゲル・ナガ族（右）の伝統衣装
Angami Naga girl (left) and Yimchunger Naga girl (right)
in their traditional dress

カシ族の伝統衣装はダハラ（黄系色の絹の上着）を纏い、
パンシニャント《銀の冠》やキークピン《金と珊瑚のネックレス》など
数種類のアクセサリーを身につける。
The Khasi traditional dress has many parts including *Ka Dhara*
(yellow or saffron colored silk cloth), *Pansngiat* (silver crown), and
*Ki Kpieng* (three rows of gold and red coral necklaces).

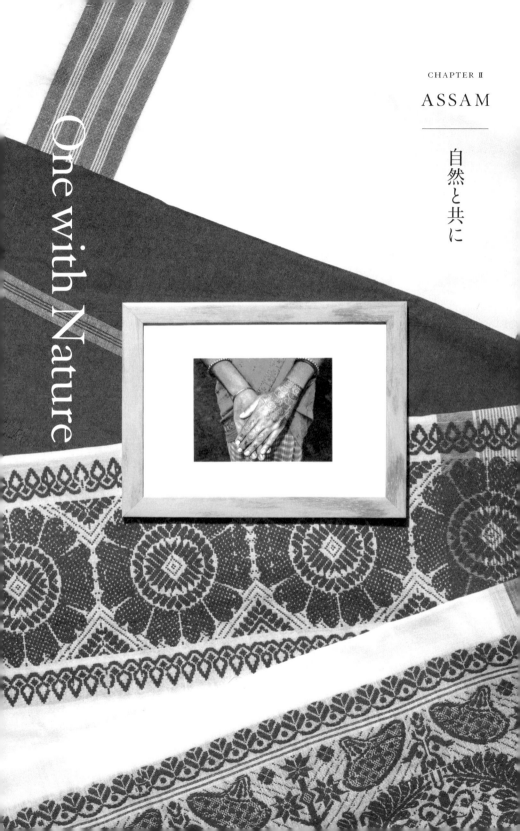

ASSAM

One with Nature

自然と共に

CHAPTER II ASSAM

CHAPTER II ASSAM

CHAPTER II          ASSAM

CHAPTER II    ASSAM

CHAPTER II ASSAM

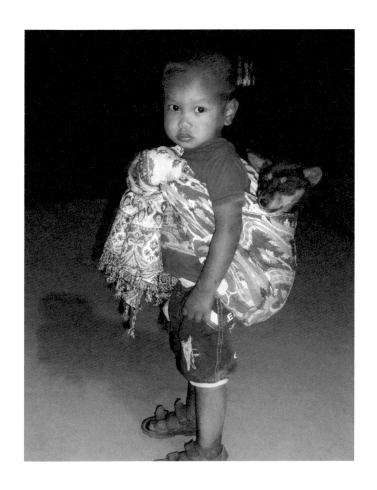

CHAPTER II ASSAM

CHAPTER II          ASSAM

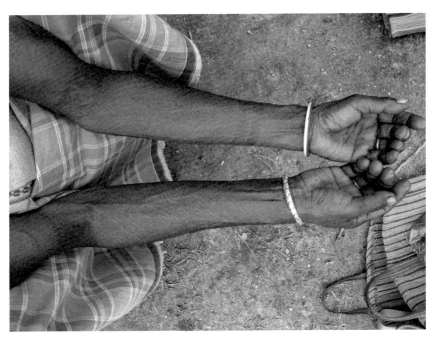

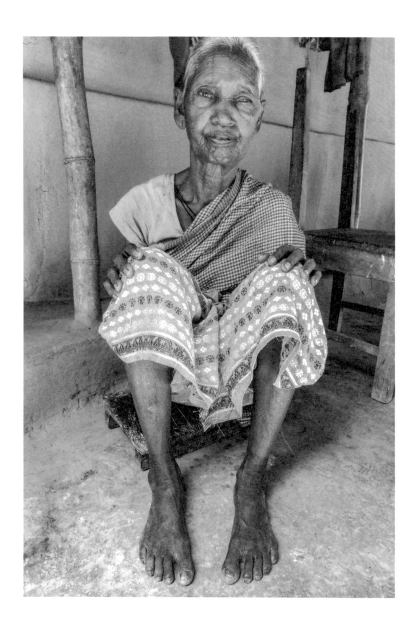

CHAPTER II    ASSAM

CHAPTER Ⅱ    A S S A M

アディバシと呼ばれる人々は19世紀、当時インドを植民地として支配していたイギリスによって、茶畑で働く契約労働者としてビハール州、ジャーカンド州、オディッサ州、西ベンガル州などからここ北東部に連れて来られた。私たちが交流しているアディバシの人々は、母語がウラオン語のウラオン族と母語がサンタリ語のサンタリ族。どちらもアッサムの共通語であるアッサム語を自由に操る。

ウラオン族のシスター・ドミニカはアッサム州カルビ・アングロングのドクムカ出身。以下は2015年に当時80歳くらいだった彼女の父上から伺ったお話だ。

「私の両親はイギリス人に『アッサムに仕事がある』と言われ、ランチ（現ジャーカンドの州都）から連れて来られた。しばらくは茶畑で牛馬のごとく働いた。私が10歳くらいの頃、新たな土地を自分たちで開墾すればそこがもらえるという話にのって移住した。それが今住んでいるこの場所だ。当時このあたり一帯はジャングルで、虎や象を含め野生動物の王国だった。蚊帳などない時代だ。野生動物から身を守る目的も兼ねて、一晩中火を焚いていた。両親は北東部に移り住む前からカトリック信者だった。ここにはたまにイタリア人の神父さまがやってきてミサをあげてくれたものだ」。

During the 19th century, Adivasi people were brought to Assam from other states including Bihar, Jharkhand, Odisha, and West Bengal as contract laborers in tea gardens of the British who ruled India at the time. Among the Adivasi, MMS are familiar with the Oraon whose Mother tongue is Oraon and the Santhali who speak Santhali. They use Assamese as well, an official language in Assam.

Sister Dominica, one of the MMS sisters from North East India belongs to the Oraon from Karbi Anglong, Assam. The following is a narrative from her late father who was around 80 years old in 2015.

"My parents were brought from Ranchi (the present day Capital city of Jharkhand state) by the British who told them that there were jobs in Assam. They worked in harsh conditions in the tea gardens for a long time. When I was about 10 years old, they decided to move here after they realized that they may be able to own land if they cultivated it themselves. The area was nothing but jungle, a paradise of wild animals, tigers and elephants included. There was no such thing as mosquito nets then. In order to protect ourselves from animals, we made fires all night long. My parents were Catholic even before they migrated here. An Italian priest used to come to say Mass once in a while."

P. 130-131

ドクムカ
Dokmoka, AS

一面に広がる田植えの時期の美しい水田。こんもり木が繁っているところに集落がある。

Beautiful rice field during the planting season. Villagers live in houses located within clusters of trees.

P. 132

スンダリ村
Sundari village, AS

牛で水田を耕し、田植えの準備をするサンタリ族の人々。

Santhali people with cows, preparing paddy fields for planting.

P. 133

スンダリ村
Sundari village, AS

サンタリ族の親子。
Santhali man and his sons.

P. 133

ドクムカ
Dokmoka, AS

伯母と甥（この子の父親はウラオン族、母親はロンマイ・ナガ族）。

Oraon woman and her nephew whose mother is Ruangmei Naga from MN and father is Oraon.

P. 134
カジャルガオン
Kajalgaon, AS
サンタリ族の女性たち。
Santhali women.

P. 134
ドクムカ
Dokmoka, AS
家の前にある大きな池で採った小魚を処理するウラオン族の女性。
Oraon woman cleaning small fish caught in a big pond in front of their house.

P. 135
ドクムカ
Dokmoka, AS
薪を集めるウラオン族の少女。
Oraon girl carrying fire wood.

P. 136
ドクムカ
Dokmoka, AS
ウラオン族の子どもたち。
Oraon children.

P. 137
ボンガイガオン
Bongaigaon, AS
教会の特別行事で踊りを披露するために伝統的なサリーを纏ったウラオン族の少女たち。

Oraon girls dressed in their cultural saree, ready to perform a traditional dance for a special parish event.

P. 137
スンダリ村
Sundari village, AS
修道院で執り行われる誓願式のために集ったサンタリ族の少女たち。MMSインド北東部本部はアッサム州のボンガイガオン教区にある。誓願式には近所からも多くの村人たちが参加した。サンタリ族とカシ族の女性が纏った極彩色の民族衣装。ノビス（修練者）たちのシ

カジャルガオン
Kajalgaon, AS
日曜日のミサに集ったサンタリ族の信者たち。ミサは太鼓の音に合わせての踊りで始まった。彼らの歌と踊りは、いわゆるインドの古典芸能とは異なる。むしろ日本の「盆踊り」のような感じで、仲間同士で輪になり列を作って歌い踊る。もちろん鳴り物入りだ。一旦始まると、これでおしまい、という気分になるまで延々と続き、時には一晩中踊り続けることもあるという。

Santhali people gathering for Sunday Mass, which started with drumming and dancing. Their dance and music is different from classical Indian performing arts. They sing and dance in a circle or in a line as a community. Once it gets started, there is no end until they feel like it's enough. Sometimes it continues all night long.

ンプルで美しいサリー姿。ミサ
でうたわれた様々な言語の聖
歌。そしてミサの後に披露され
た民族ダンスのオンパレード。こ
の日の様子をライブでお届けで
きないのがとても残念。

Santhali girls in a formal dress.
The MMS Provincial house is
in Sundari which belongs to
the Bongaigaon Diocese.
Many villagers joined us on the
special occasion of profession
of religious vows for our sister.
It was a colorful and joyous
scene to admire: women in
their brilliant traditional
attire, our novices in beauti-
fully simple sarees, and songs
sung in different languages.
The highlight was various
tribal dances performed on
parade. How I wish I could
show you what I saw that day!

P. 138
ドクムカ
Dokmoka, AS
顔に刺青のあるカルビ族の女
性。

Karbi woman with tattoo
on her face.

P. 139
ドクムカ
Dokmoka, AS
自宅の前に並ぶカルビ族の家
族。

Karbi family in front of
their house.

P. 140-141
ドクムカ
Dokmoka, AS
家族に朝ご飯をよそうカルビ
族の女性。

Karbi woman serving
breakfast to her family.

P. 142
ボンガイガオン
Bongaigaon, AS
ヤギ肉売り場。
Goat meat section.

P. 143
ドクムカ
Dokmoka, AS
このカルビ族の男の子は兄弟
姉妹いとこの中で一番の年下。
ある日、日が沈んであたりが
薄暗くなった夕方に、子犬をまる
で弟のようにおんぶした姿
で現れた。ほどなくして食事の
時間になるとそのまま土間に
座り、背中におぶった子犬に
食べさせ始めた。子犬はという
と、とりわけ嫌がるふうもなく
おとなしく食べさせてもらうの
だった。

私が家庭訪問で歩き回ったインド北東部には、スタジ
オジブリの映画を彷彿とさせる風景がたくさんある。
アッサム州のドクムカを訪ねた時のこと。ちょうどディワリ
というヒンズー教のお祭りの時期で、暗くなるとあちらこ
ちらの家には小さな素焼きのお皿にいくつものランプが
灯されていた。アッサム州もまた何かと情勢が不安定に
なりがちだが、そんな現実とは裏腹にとても穏やかな夜
だった。小川のほとりではたくさんの蛍が飛び交ってい
る。一緒に歩いていた生徒がひゅうっと捕まえた。私に
見せようとそおっと開いた手のひらをのぞき込むと、柔ら
かい光が優しく輝いていた。

A few years back, I visited the village of Dokmoka, Assam. It was
Diwali season, a very popular
Hindu Festival, and people light
many lamps on small earthen plates
in front of their homes. Along the
creek, plenty of fireflies flew in the
dark. The scene was just so lovely
and familiar to me. Catching it
swiftly and opening it in her hand
ever so gently, our student showed
me a firefly radiating its bright light
in the darkness.

ドクムカ
Dokmoka, AS

カルビ族の少年と犬。犬はどの家でも門番として欠かせない存在。もちろん大事な家族の一員だ。

Karbi boy and his dog. People in the area keep dogs in their compounds. They are watch dogs, and even more, loyal companions who are important members of the family.

This Karbi boy is the youngest among his siblings and cousins. One day after sunset, he appeared with a puppy on his back. As his aunt called for supper, he went into the kitchen with him, sat on the floor and began to feed him while on his back. The dog didn't make any fuss over it and seemed willing to be treated as his younger brother.

P. 144-145
カルビ・アングロング
Karbi Anglong, AS

カルビ・アングロングにある学校を訪問した。子どもたちはアッサム人、ベンガル人、ネパール人、カルビ族と実に様々。授業はすべて英語だが、休み時間にはお互いにいくつもの異なる言語を自由に話す。「シスターは？英語だけなの？」と聞かれたので、あたふたと何語をどれくらい話せるかを説明し、「でももちろん、日本語はバッチリよ！」と言ってから、とんだ当たり前のことを言ったと我ながら苦笑いした。

One day, I visited a school in Karbi Anglong. Pupils belong to several ethnic groups such as Assamese, Bengali, Nepali, and Karbi. They use English in the class, but at break time I heard various languages spoken among them. They have incredible command of different languages, indeed! "How about you, sister? Do you speak only English?" they asked. Explaining that I barely manage a few languages other than English, I concluded with a remark "You know what, I speak Japanese perfectly!" Oh, well...

P. 146-147
ドクムカ
Dokmoka, AS

ある暑い夏の日、シスター・ドミニカの母上のお葬式に参列した。田植えで大忙しの時期だが村の人々はこの日仕事を休み、共に悼むためにドミニカの家に集った。神父である親戚が到着するのを待つ間、女性たちは安置されたご遺体のそばに沈黙のうちに座り、男性たちは手際よく棺桶を作り葬儀の準備を進めていった。家の敷地内でミサが捧げられた後、じりじりと太陽が照りつける中を参列者全員で近くの墓地まで見送った。

One hot summer day, I attended the funeral of Sister Dominica's mother. Though busy with planting, the villagers did not go to the field that day in order to mourn together at her house. While waiting for the arrival of her nephew who is a priest, women sat around the mother in silence and men made a coffin and prepared for the funeral outside. After Mass on the front yard of the house, we all walked under the blazing sun to the graveyard to bid farewell.

157

サンタリ族の人々は相手によって異なる挨拶をする。
とても微笑ましく、愛らしい仕草だ。
Santhali people have different styles of greetings according to the situation.
In any case, it is very gracious and sometimes just so sweet!

年上の女性が年下の女性に。
Elder woman to younger one.

年下の女性が年上の女性に。
Younger woman to elder one.

妻が夫に。
Wife to husband.

少年が年上の男性に。
Young boy to elder man.

少年が年上の女性に。
Young boy to elder woman.

花嫁と花婿の母親同士。
Mothers of a bride and bridegroom.

花嫁の母親と花婿の父親。
Mother of a bride and father of a bridegroom.

花嫁と花婿の父親同士。
Fathers of a bride and bridegroom.

P. 148
スンダリ村
Sundari village, AS
挨拶をするサンタリ族の女性
たち。
Santhali women greeting
each other.

P. 149–151
ボンガイガオン
Bongaigaon, AS
サンタリ族の女性の刺青。
Tattoos on bodies of
Santhali women.

P. 152
ドクムカ
Dokmoka, AS
シスター・ドミニカの母上。ウラ
オン族の女性はこの世代まで
刺青をしていた。身元証明のた
めに始まったのが、次第に「み
んながしているから…」という
具合に広まっていったという。
その刺青はアクセサリーの代

わりにもなった。首飾り、腕輪、
足輪……腕全体に刺青を施し
た人もいる。年齢を重ねるにつ
れて色は褪せていくが、当初は
まことに鮮やかな青だった。

Mother of Sister Dominica.
The women of the Oraon
used to have tattoos, up to the
generation of Sr Dominica's
mother. Originally it was for
self-identity. Tattoos were
also a substitute for accessories such as a necklace, a
wrist ring or an ankle ring.
Some women had their
whole arms covered with
intricate designs. As they
age, the color fades and
women claim that original
tattoos used to be a brilliant
blue color.

スンダリ村
Sundari village, AS
米の苗を運ぶサンタリ族の女性。田植えは炎天下での仕事だ。
日傘は欠かせない。
Santhali woman carrying rice plants. They spend a whole
day in the field under the scorching sun for planting. An
umbrella is a must item as a protection from the heat.

# Tapestry of Life

CHAPTER III    GARO

CHAPTER III        GARO

CHAPTER III   GARO

CHAPTER III    GARO

CHAPTER III    GARO

CHAPTER III     GARO

CHAPTER Ⅲ    G A R O

言い伝え

ガロヒルズのモナバリ村では、一人の女性から象にまつわるいくつかのお話を聞きました。「この村にはね、収穫の季節になると、子象、若象、大きな象あわせて40から50頭くらいがやってきて、たわわに実った稲を食べてしまうことがあるの。でもそれも日常生活の一部。仕方ないわ」「少し前にはね、夜に電柱の周りで遊んでいた子象が7頭も感電して死んでしまったの。かわいそうだった、ほんとに。妊娠7ヶ月の人が象の恨みを買って襲われたこともあった。象は鼻を上手に操って胎児を安全に取り出した後、妊婦さんを踏み潰して森に戻っていったって聞いたわ。その人、いつも象についてあれこれ文句を言っていたんですって」。

同じくガロヒルズのスロプグレ村では、こんなお話も聞きました。「あっちのジャングルにある大きな池には不思議な生き物がいて、なんでも食べてしまうんだ。だから村人は死んだ犬やら牛やらをその池の中に捨てる。池の中にはたくさん魚がいるから、釣ってもいいけれど、食べるんだったらそこで食べること。家に持ち帰って食べたりなんかすると、体が溶けて骸骨になってしまうよ！」。

もう一つ、ナガ民族が住んでいるマニプール州で聞いた不

思議なお話。「ある豚が出産した。その時、なんと豚の赤ちゃんと一緒に、象、馬、猿が一頭ずつ生まれてきた。後になってその母豚を食べることになったのだけれど、食べた人は皆、豚に宿っていた悪霊の仕業で肉にあたって死んでしまった」ということです。話してくれた人が「出産しているところを実際に僕も見た」と真顔で言っていました。ほんとですかね？

# Narratives

In the village of Monabari, Garo Hills, one lady told me some stories of elephants. "Sometimes during the harvest season, a herd of elephants–small, medium and large, about 40 to 50 will come to the village and almost finish the abundant paddies. Well, such is life," she said philosophically. Continuing, she recounted two more tales. "A while ago, seven baby elephants were electrocuted when playing near the electric poles at night. Poor souls, indeed! I felt such pity." "Another time, a seven months pregnant woman was attacked by an elephant. It manipulated its trunk amazingly, took out the fetus from her womb intact, crushed her and returned to the jungle! You know what? That woman was known to complain about the elephants every so often. She must have incurred their enmity."

From Garo Hills comes another story: "There lives a mysterious creature in a big pond in the jungle over there. It eats anything, so the villagers discard all sorts of things including dead bodies of dogs and buffalos. You can fish there as there are plenty of fish. However, I will warn you. You have to eat what you catch there. If you take it home and eat the fish, your entire body gets dissolved and you become a skeleton!"

I heard another strange story in Manipur where the Naga people reside. They say that at one time, a pig delivered piglets–along with one elephant, one horse and one monkey! Nonetheless, after some time the villagers ate the mother pig. They say that all who ate the meat died of food poisoning by the evil spirit in the pig! The person who told me the story said, "I too witnessed the delivery. I swear!" What do you think?

P. 170
ガロヒルズ
Garo Hills, ML
郷愁をそそる田園風景。
Rural scenery reminding of
home land.

P. 170
ガロヒルズ
Garo Hills, ML
収穫した稲穂と自転車。
Bundles of rice just har-
vested from a paddy and
loaded on a bicycle.

P. 171
スロプグレ村
Sropgre village, ML
ガロの親子。男の子はカメラを
怖がって背を向けてしまった。
Garo family. Noticing that I
was watching from afar
with a camera, the boy was
scared and turned his back
to me. Sorry, dear!

P. 172
スロプグレ村
Sropgre village, ML

家でくつろぐガロの女性。
Garo woman relaxing at
home.

P. 173
コイクリ村
Koikuri village, ML
孫と飼い犬を抱くガロの男性。
Garo man holding his
grandson and dog.

P. 174
ラジャバラ村
Rajabala village, ML
収穫したもみ米を運ぶガロの
親子。
Garo mother and son carrying a sack of threshed rice.

P. 175
ラジャバラ村
Rajabala village, ML
もみ米の入った麻袋を自転車
に積み終わったガロの夫婦。
Garo couple with sacks of
threshed rice.

P. 176
ラジャバラ村
Rajabala village, ML
風で実入りの悪い稲穂を飛散
させて良い稲穂を選別する（風
選）ガロの女性。
Winnowing Garo woman.

P. 177
ラジャバラ村
Rajabala village, ML
穫り入れをするガロの女性たち。
Garo women harvesting
rice.

P. 177
ラジャバラ村
Rajabala village, ML
赤ん坊を背負って収穫したも
み米をまとめるガロの女性。
Garo woman gathering rice
after it has been threshed.
Her baby sleeps contentedly
on her back.

P. 178
ガロヒルズ
Garo Hills, ML

川に仕掛けられたいくつもの
大きな四つ手網。

Numerous huge four armed
scoop nets set in the river.

P. 179
ラジャバラ村
Rajabala village, ML

ガロヒルズでは雨季になると乾
季には陸地のところにも水が溜
まり、絶好の魚釣り場になる。
籠はペットボトルで沈まないよう
工夫されていた。ここでは他に
も、日本ではすぐに捨てられて
ゴミになるプラスチックの容器が
入れ物としてとても重宝される。

During rainy season in
Garo Hills, fields trans-
formed into excellent fishing
ponds. People attached plastic bottles to a basket in such
a way that it does not sink.
Various plastic containers
which are considered trash
in Japan find good alterna-
tive ways to be reused here.

P. 180
ラジャバラ村
Rajabala village, ML
姉の息子を抱くガロの兄弟。

Garo brothers carrying their
elder sister's sons.

ガロヒルズ
Garo Hills, ML

バナナの木でいかだを作り、水遊びに興じるガロの少年たち。数
年前、ガロヒルズでも武装集団が若者を洗脳してそれがキノコの
ようにどんどん増え、治安が著しく悪化した時期があった。こうい
う幼気な少年たちが巻き込まれたケースもあったかもしれない。
幸いに、シャローム・メガラヤというガロヒルズのカトリック教会が
呼びかけて広まった平和運動が効を奏して事態は鎮静化した。

Garo boys playing in the paddy field with a boat made of
banana trees. Some years back, militants brainwashed the
young in Garo Hills to increase their ranks, and they grew
like mushrooms after the rain. The security situation had
gotten worse in Garo Hills and the tense atmosphere was
tangible at that time. Innocent boys like them may have been
lured by such groups. Fortunately, the peace program called
Shalom Meghalaya, initiated by Catholic Church in Garo
Hills, was very successful to quiet down such anti-social
activities in the area.

P. 181
コイクリ村
Koikuri village, ML
ガロの祖母と孫たち。先生だっ
たコニカさんには4人の娘と6
人の息子がいて、娘夫婦はもち
ろん、6人のうち4人の息子夫
婦もまた彼女の家の敷地内に
住んでいる。まるで小さな村の
ような大家族だ。お嫁さんたち
はバプティストだったので、婿
になった息子たちがカトリック
からバプティストに改宗するの
を猛反対して、自分のところに
呼び寄せたのだとか。

Garo grandmother and
granddaughters. Mrs.
Konica is a mother of four
daughters and six sons. All
her daughters' and four of
her sons' families reside on
her property. The extended
family is like a village itself!

ガロヒルズのある村には樹齢300年以上の大きな木が何本もあるが、雨はそういう木があるところにまず降るという。木漏れ日があたりを輝かせる中で様々な鳥がさえずり、まるでユートピアのようだった。お昼過ぎになって道に出ると、ガンティという虫が放つ警戒速報のようなピーッという高いピッチの金属音がかなり強烈な音量で響いていた。

波羅蜜やマンゴーやライチやサポジラなど、様々な果樹が豊かに茂るジャングルがまだ残っているガロヒルズ。近年は手っ取り早い換金作物であるビンロウやゴムの木がどんどん植えられている。その村にはちゃんと保護区域が設けてあり、それを侵すと罰金は5,000ルピー（約7,500円）と牛一頭だそう。それでもやはり植生は変わっていってしまうのではないのだろうか。

In the village there are huge trees which are over 300 years old. They say the rain starts from those trees. The surroundings were like a utopia, birds chipping here and there between the gentle rays of the Sun. We came out of the woods to a main road. There, an insect called *ganti* was making peculiar sounds very loudly like an alarm.

Garo Hills are blessed with forests where various fruit trees such as Jackfruits, Mangos, Lychee and *Chikoo* grow. Lately, however, villagers are planting cash crops like betel and rubber trees more and more. The village as a result has its own rules and penalties for violating lands that are protected, it is said that fines can include a cow and 5,000 rupees. However, the vegetation may not be the same in the future.

p. 182–183

ラジャバラ村

Rajabala village, ML

同じ民族でも顔つきはいろいろだ。ガロの人々も然り。週に一度の市場に行くと、私たちの修道院の周りでは普段あまり見かけない顔に出会う。彼らはもっと人里離れたところに住んでいると聞いた。

There certainly are different faces among members of a same tribe. So it is with the Garo. In weekly markets in Garo Hills, I see faces which are not so common around areas where MMS live. I heard that these people would come from more remote places in the hills.

..............................

p. 184–185

ラジャバラ村

Rajabala village, ML

ベンガリの牛飼いの青年。

Bengali young man taking care of buffaloes.

..............................

p. 186

キットキパラ村

Kitkipara village, ML

ハジョン族の子どもたち。ハジョン族はヒンズー教徒か精霊信仰者。

Hajong children. Hajong people are Hindus or Animists.

P. 187
カルパラ村
Kalpara village, ML

ビンロウの実を剥くコッチ族の
女性。ハジョン族とコッチ族の
人々はよく似ていて見分けがつ
きにくいらしい。

Koch woman skinning areca
nut. The features of Hajong
and Koch are very similar
and difficult to distinguish
even for Garo people.

P. 188
ラジャバラ村
Rajabala village, ML

雨季と乾季のサイクルがおか
しくなってきている。大雨で畦
道も使えなくなり、急遽、竹を
田んぼに渡らせてその上を歩
いて稲刈りに向かうガロの女
性たち。

The rain cycles and dry sea-
sons have been unusual in
Garo Hills as well because
of Climate Change. They
had out of season heavy rain
and a path between rice
fields became useless. They
made a temporary "road"
with bamboo sticks to reach
the paddy fields to harvest.

P. 189
ラジャバラ村
Rajabala village, ML

道路整備の日雇い労働をするベ
ンガリとハジョン族の女性たち。

Bengali and Hajong women
engaged in daily wage labor.

P. 189
コイクリ村
Koikuri village, ML

田んぼから戻ってきたいくつ
かの部族の女性たち。5月な
のに季節外れの大雨で、実っ
た稲穂を刈り入れるのも、腰
まで水に浸かりながらの作業
だ。これ以上被害が出ないよ
う、時間との勝負だと村人は嘆
いていた。

Women who belong to dif-
ferent ethnic groups coming
back from the paddy fields.
Unseasonable heavy rain in
May makes their work even
harder because the water in
the field comes up to their
waists. They are pressed for
time to harvest rice as fast as
possible to minimize the
damage.

---

メガラヤ州はインド国内で最も降水量の多い地域だという。サ
ンスクリット語で「メガ」は「雲」、「ア・ラヤ」は「すみか」を意味
する名前の所以だ。ガロヒルズは実に水が豊富で、チダリとい
う竹で作られた水を集める仕掛けが森のあちこちにある。し
かし、地球全体が気候変動の危機に直面している現在、ガロ
ヒルズも例外ではない。メンディパタでは数年前に井戸の水が
いっとき枯れてしまった。80歳くらいのおばあさんは「こんなこ
とは生まれて初めて！」と、起こり得ないことが起きたと言わん
ばかりに驚いていた。

"Meghalaya" means "abode of clouds" in Sanskrit and
they say the state of Meghalaya has the highest amount of
rainfall in India. Thus Garo Hills have abundant water.
It is common to see their traditional bamboo water collec-
tor called *Chidari* in the woods. However, now that the
whole earth is in climate crisis, Garo Hills is not an excep-
tion. One year wells in Mendipathar were dried up. An
old lady who was almost in her 80s was simply stunned at
this sudden change, saying, "Very first time in my life!"

P. 190–191

ラジャバラ村
Rajabala village, ML

季節外れの大雨でせっかく実った稲穂が台無しになってしまった。それでもなんとか刈り取って、牛に踏ませての脱穀作業をする。

The out of season heavy rains have ruined the ears of rice that have grown. Even so, they managed to cut them and let the cows step on them to continue the threshing process.

P. 192

ガズン村
Gajing village, ML

ガズン村
Gajing village, ML

両親、娘と息子それぞれ6人のガロの家族。中央に写る母親の右隣に座っているのは息子の一人サムエル。乗っていたバスの屋根から転落して右半身が不自由になった。ガロは女系社会で、結婚すると男性は妻の村に住む。事故の後、サムエルは居づらくなったのだろう、妻と子ども2人を残して実家に戻ってきた。私は彼の鍼治療にせっせと通ったが、そのたびに苦労をいとわず献身的にサムエルを介護する家族の姿には深く心を動かされた。

A Garo family, mother, father, six girls and six boys. In the second row, the man sitting next to the right of mother is Samuel, one of their six sons. He had an accident falling from the top of a moving bus and became half paralyzed. Garo have a matrilineal society, and a husband lives in the wife's village. Samuel had married a woman with two children. After the accident, he came back to his own village by himself and his family continues to care for him very lovingly.

おめかしをしたガロの少女。ガロの青年が数年間の準備期間を終えていよいよ神父になるという、特別な儀式が執り行われる日。とっておきのおめかしをした親族一同が家に集まる。結婚式のような祝宴には、200人以上にもなる参加者が家に招かれた。出し物はすべて自前。数日前から料理する場所を用意し、数頭の牛や豚、何十羽という鶏を屠り、魚を市場で買い、下準備をする。お米も大量に炊き上げて、一人前ずつバナナの葉で包む。会場となる教会と家の敷地一帯のデコレーションもしなければならない。女性も男性も子どもも皆それぞれに貢献し、気分はどんどん盛り上がっていくのだった。

Dressed up Garo girl. It is a day of the Priestly Ordination. All the family members and relatives were gathered together to celebrate this auspicious occasion. More than 200 people were invited to the feast. They spent days prior preparing the food to be served - several cows, pigs, dozens of chickens and fish from the market, as well as a very large amount of cooked rice to be packed in banana leaves. Besides that, decorations had to be put out on the whole property of the church and the house. All contributed in one way or another and the atmosphere was getting merrier and merrier.

チュムケディマの市場で鶏を売るベンガリの女性
Bengali woman selling chickens at market in Chumukedima

ナガランド州チュムケディマの市場
Market in Chumukedima, NL

ナガオニオン（らっきょう）
Scallions

左＝ナガ名産の唐辛子、右＝茄子
Left: Naga's special chili  Right: Brinjal

地元でラジャチリ（ラジャは王様、チリは唐辛子）と呼ばれる激辛唐辛子。他の唐辛子よりはるかに値が張り、近頃は15個で100ルピー（約150円）する。

Raja (meaning king) chili is extremely hot and much more expensive than the other chilis. This day we paid 100 rupees for fifteen pieces of King chili while ordinary kinds were 100 rupees for 1kg.

## 納豆
### Fermented soybeans

インド北東部に住む民族・部族は様々だが、食生活には共通点がたくさんある。アクニと呼ばれる納豆はその一つ。このまま食べるのではなく、調味料やチャトニーというご飯のお供の材料として使う。アクニ、生姜、干し魚、唐辛子などを混ぜ合わせて作ったチャトニーさえあれば、いくらでもご飯が食べられる。たとえ時間が経って大豆の形がなくなり真っ黒な塊になっても全然大丈夫。むしろコクが出てますますいい感じになる。発酵食品は他にもよく使われ、中でもケセという発酵させた筍は定番。

There are various ethnic groups in North East India, and they have lots of commonalities in eating habits, which are also similar to those of South East and East Asia. *Akhuni* (fermented soybeans, *Natto* in Japanese) is one of them. Other fermented food, especially *Kese* (fermented bamboo) is popular in the region.

山のような唐辛子。ナガの食事はおおむね辛い。
Mountains of chili. Naga food is hot in general.

**ヨングチャキ・カンバ**
*Yongchaki Kanba*

これは私にとって、なんでも工夫して食べようとするナガの人々の創意工夫を感じる食材の一つ。チャトニーとして使う場合、硬い外皮をこそぎ落としてから薄く斜め切りにする。それに紫玉ねぎの薄切りと干し魚、にんにく、生姜、唐辛子を混ぜてペースト状にしたものを和えて出来あがり。薬としても様々な効用があるらしい。

To me this is one of the typical examples which shows the creativity and zeal of the Naga people: to eat whatever the earth provides. The outer skin is so hard that you have to scrape it off first and cut into thin slices. To make chutney, you mix it with thinly sliced red onions, minced garlic, ginger and hot pepper. Not to mention it has quite a few medicinal qualities as well.

多種多様な乾燥した魚
Various dried fish

### 蜂の子
### Wasp

季節になると国道沿いにまで出店が出る。一山 2,000 – 3,000 ルピー（約 3,000 – 4,500 円）と高価だがよく売れる。

Wasp is one of the favorite seasonal delicacies for the Naga people. It sells well in spite of its high price (about 2,000–3,000 rupees for one pile).

カタツムリ
Snail

乾燥した魚
Dried fish

魚を売るボド族の女性
Bodo woman selling fish

市場には様々な甲虫や毛虫も売られている。これは地中に生息する甲虫。表面の黒く硬い羽はむしってある。

In a market, various insects are available. This is called *Pfuteo* in Angami language. It belongs to Beetles family found underground. The outer hard wing is cut off.

乾燥ウナギはとても高価な食材で、1キロあたり500ルピー（約750円）。主にマニプリの人々が食するそうだ。

Dried eel fish is an expensive food stuff mainly used by Manipuri people. It costs 500 rupees per 1kg.

マイブラと呼ばれる地酒の素を売るボド族の女性たち。米粉に薬草を加え、発酵させて団子状にしたもので、ネパールで使われる餅麹とよく似ている。

Bodo women selling starter called *Maibra* to make local liquor. It is made of rice powder and herbs. It is very similar to the one called *Murcha* in Nepal.

左＝蚕、右＝カエル

Left: Silk worms　Right: Frogs

カエルが出てくる季節には、蚕の幼虫やタガメや小さい黒いカタツムリと並んで体長15センチくらいのカエルが売られている。カエルのスープは絶品で、滋養強壮にも最適とか。

When the season comes, frogs are available along with silk worms, snails and giant water bugs at the market. They say soup made out of frogs is exquisite and supplies good nutrients.

ボド族の女性が纏う色鮮やかなドコナを売るボド族の女性たち
Bodo women selling colorful Bodo's cloth called *dokhona*

ディマプールとコヒマ間の国道沿いに常時ある出店。
白い品物が発酵筍のケセ。

Shop at the National highway between Kohima and
Dimapur. The white stuff is fermented bamboo shoots.

Treasures in Relationship

CHAPTER IV    KHASI

CHAPTER IV          KHASI

CHAPTER IV        KHASI

CHAPTER IV KHASI

CHAPTER IV    K H A S I

## 市場でのこと

土曜日は週に一度の市が立つ日。活気があって、エキゾチックなものがいっぱいあって、いつ行ってもわくわくします。ある時、いつもは避ける肉売り場にも足を運んでみたのですが、目にした光景はやはりかなり強烈でした。悲鳴かと思ってしまうような豚の鳴き声が遠くから聞こえるので恐る恐る近づいてみると、麻袋が数えきれないほど転がっていてブヒブヒ鳴きながらモゾモゾ動いています。出されたのはきれいな黒い子豚でした。

その横の売り場には鶏たちが声ひとつ上げずにじっと地面に蹲っています。そこを過ぎると四つ足肉売り場。まず目に飛び込んできたのは、台の上に置かれている立派なミトゥン（ナガランド固有種の牛）の頭でした。台の下にも動物の頭があちこちに（その中には皮を剥がされたものも…）。さらに奥に入ると、ちょうど豚の頭を大きな鉈で叩き切っているところでした。あたり一帯は、台に並べられたものを触ったり持ち上げたりして、

注意深く見定めては買っていく人々で大変な混みようです。実に衝撃的でした。しかし考えてみれば、数年前友人に案内してもらった築地市場でも、人目を引くために大層立派なマグロの頭が飾られていたし、床にはやっぱりあちこちにマグロの頭が放置されていました。大きな包丁でマグロの頭を切り分けるのも、うなぎの捌き方にしても然り、初めて見る人にしてみれば仰天する光景かもしれません。

## Market Scenes

Every Saturday, there is an open market in the village. It is always so vibrant with lots of activities. I remember it was filled with things that were exotic to my eyes and experience. Usually I avoided the meat section, but one time I decided to take a look. What I observed was quite astonishing. From far, I heard the squealing of pigs. Fearfully I approached the area to find numerous jute bags that moving with animal grunts coming from them. When the contents of the bags were revealed, there were beautiful shiny black piglets. Next to it, I saw chickens crouching silently, lined up to be sold. Passing further along, I saw a section for four-legged animal meat. Right at the front, the head of a *Mithun* (A unique kind of buffalo which inhabits Nagaland) appeared before my eyes. Under the stand, there were more heads lying around. Some of them were even skinless. Proceeding, I came across a man with a large knife chopping the head of a pig. Around the area, there was a huge crowd of people choosing which piece to buy.

I found myself astonished at the whole scene. However, on reflection, I realized that I had observed something similar at a famous fish market in Tokyo: There, a large tuna head was put on display to attract visitors. There were other heads of tunas lying on the ground as well. I imagine the scene may have also been rather shocking for foreigners who visited Japan.

P. 210

シロン
Shillong, ML

シロンの市場では、労働者が一目でかなりの重量だとわかる様々なものを担いで、人混みの中を巧みに足早に行き交う姿をよく見る。2メートルはあろうスチールロッカーや大きな肉の塊さえも担ぐところを見たこともあった。実に過酷な労働だ。彼らは屈強でその表情は非常に険しく、今でも脳裏に焼き付いている。

In a market place in Shillong, it is common to see laborers carrying all kinds of heavy items on their backs and go up and down the street at a very quick pace. One time I saw a man carrying a steel locker of 2 meters high. Another time, humongous chunks of meat. Hard work, indeed. Their body structure is stalwart and their expression is intense, and I find it haunting.

P. 211

シロン
Shillong, ML

ここでは様々な方面に向かう乗合タクシーが次から次へと通り過ぎていく。行き先がどこかに表示されているわけではないので、人々はタクシーが来るたびに運転手に尋ねることになる。運が良ければ1回、悪

ければ果てしなくだ。日本のタクシーよりずっと小型だが、その許容量は驚くべきもの。運転手は必要とあらば自分の隣に乗客を二人座らせ、体を横にねじって運転する。後部座席では、乗客は前と後の交互にお尻をずらして座る。ある時にはなんと文字通り体を直角に曲げて乗る人がいた。そうなると「乗る」というより「入っている」感じだ。数えてみると私を含め乗客は11人だった。

Shared taxis heading towards various destinations come and go at this junction. Since there are no signs on the taxis, people ask a driver where the vehicle is going whenever one passes by. If you are lucky, you only need to ask once, but if not, it can be an endless trial to find your transport. It is much smaller than a taxi in Japan, but the capacity is astonishing. A driver lets one or even two passengers sit next to him on a driver's seat, which makes him twist his upper body to enable him to drive. In the back seat, passengers sit in all types of positions contorting their bodies to fit into the vehicle. Once, a passenger bent her body 90 degrees just to be inside the vehicle, but she was not sitting! The total number of the passengers was 11 including myself.

P. 212

チェラプンジ
Cherrapunji, ML

炭鉱の跡地。メガラヤ州は炭鉱が豊富で、カシの男性の多くは出稼ぎで働いていた。ところが、2014年にナショナル・グリーン・トリビューナル・アクト

シロン
Shillong, ML
市場の一角で見た裁縫師。
Tailors at a corner in a market.

チェラプンジ

Cherrapunji, ML

チェラプンジは、イギリス・ウェールズの長老派宣教師が1841年に初めてバングラデシュ側から入ってきた場所。ちなみにカシ語に英語のアルファベットを当てはめたのは、トマス・ジョーンズという宣教師だった。

In 1841, the first Presbyterian missionary of Wales entered Khasi Hills from Bangladesh. It is Thomas Jones, one of the missionaries, who wrote Khasi language in the Latin script.

（国家グリーン審判所法）によってメガラヤ州のすべての炭鉱が突然閉鎖されてしまい、「大事な現金収入が途絶えて家族をはじめ村人は皆とても困っている」とカシヒルズ出身のシスターから聞いた。そういえば、シロンとグワハティを結ぶ国道を石炭運搬するトラックが盛んに行き来していたが、それもすっかり見なくなった。

Ruins of coal mines. Meghalaya state is rich in coal mines and Khasi men used to work there. However, in 2014, all the mines in the state were closed because of the National Green Tribunal Act. Our sister from Khasi Hills told me that the people have been negatively impacted because a major income source is cut off all of the sudden.

P. 213
ダウキ

Dawki, ML

勧誘活動の新天地を開拓しようとバングラデシュとの国境に近いダウキまで足をのばした。乗合タクシーは標高の高いカシヒルズからどんどん下りていく。ふと窓の外を見下ろすと、意外な光景が目に飛び込んできた。ここは地元の人たちにも人気のある観光地、ということは、あそこは湖水浴場みたいなところなのだろうか。

To explore a new area for vocation promotion, we went by shared taxi to Dawki near the border of Bangladesh. We drove down from the highlands of Khasi Hills. As we approached Dawki, I was taken by surprise at the scene from the vehicle. It seemed like a lakeside beach and then I remembered people had told me about the area, saying it is very popular among the local people.

P. 214–215
シロン

Shillong, ML

シロンはメガラヤ州の州都。高地にあり、昔からイギリス軍とインド軍、そして海外からの宣教師たちの避暑地として人気があった。メガラヤ州はキリスト教が盛んで、シロンの中心部には多くのミッションスクールに囲まれた大きなカテドラルがある。ムスリムもヒンズー教徒もほとんど見かけないというのはインドではかなり珍しいだろう。市が立ちトラックや乗合タクシーやバスが所狭しと引っ切りなしに行き来する繁華街は、極めてアジア的に種々雑多で活力があり、物珍しい光景が随所に見られる。

Shillong is the Capital of the state of Meghalaya. It was a popular hill station for both the British and the Indian army as well as overseas missionaries. Meghalaya being a Christian state, there is a grand Cathedral surrounded by many missionary schools at the center of Shillong. It is rather rare in India not to see any Hindus and Muslims in the town. Downtown Shillong is full of life with exotic bazaars, heavy traffic and very interesting scenes at every corner.

P. 216
マウブリ村
Mawbri village, ML
猫は鼠対策としてどの家でも飼われている。

They keep cats as mouse deterrents at every household.

P. 217
マウラスナイ村
Mawlasnai village, ML
生姜を収穫した青年たち。

Young men on the way from harvesting ginger from the field.

P. 218
マウカルワット村
Mawkyrwat village, ML
ここには公園なんてないのだが、彼らにとってはどこも遊び場になる。家庭訪問する私と案内してくれた二人の生徒の後を面白がってついてきた弟たち。通りかかった建築現場でも格好の遊び道具を見つけていた。

Khasi children. There is no such thing as parks in the area, but for children it does not matter as they make anywhere their playground. These are our students' brothers following us to visit families.

P. 219
ラミン村
Lamin village, ML
台所に立つカシの少女。カシの女性は、家ではいつもエプロンをするように肩から布を掛けている。カシは小柄な人が多い。

Young Khasi woman in the kitchen. Khasi women always wear a characteristic apron in the house. In general, Khasi people are small in size.

P. 220
ラミン村
Lamin village, ML
ビンロウを市場に持っていくカシの女性。

Khasi woman carrying areca nuts to take them to a market.

P. 221
マウカルワット村
Mawkyrwat village, ML
食堂で売るおかず(魚の頭を辛く煮込んだもの)を見せてくれるカシの女性の口はクワイで赤く染まっていた。

The mouth of woman whom I met at a diner in a village was red because of *Kwai*.

P. 221
マウブリ村
Mawbri village, ML
クワイのセットとそれ用のシャン・クワイと呼ばれる籠。

Areca nuts, betel leaves, paste of lime and a knife put in a basket called *Shangkwai* to prepare *Kwai*.

.........................................

P. 222

ライトレンコット村
Laitlyngkot village, ML
カシヒルズの南、バングラデシュが見渡せるラミン村からの帰りの道中でご当地名物、豚の腸と血でできたド・スニャル・スナムというソーセージを食べる機会があった。「さあシスター、食べて食べて、元気が出るよ！」と勧められては断るわけにもいかない。覚悟を決めて口にすると結構いけるではないか。差し出された生の紫玉ねぎと一緒に食べてみると、もっとおいしい。その上、確かに力が湧いてきた気がした。

On the way back from Lamin village close to the border with Bangladesh, I had a chance to taste their local speciality: a blood sausage called *Doh Snier Snam* made with pig intestine. I could not say no to his friendly offer and tried one bite nervously. Surprisingly I enjoyed it! It was tastier with a few slices of raw red onion. In fact, I found myself feeling stronger after eating this.

マウカルワット村
Mawkyrwat village, ML

鶏の下ごしらえをするカシ族の家族。シスター・ファーストリー・メアリー（写真左から2番目）はMMSのカシ族シスター第1号。当初、私は彼女たちと接しながらカシ文化を少しずつ学んでいった。カシ族には一風変わった名前が多い。カトリックでメアリーは普通すぎる女の子の名前だが、彼女の場合、長女として生まれたので一番という意味の英語をもじった「ファーストリー」がメアリーの前につけられたのだそう。ジョイフル・メアリーという名前も聞いたことがある。お客が来たということで、特別な夕飯を用意する。食事を準備するのは日本でいうと土間のようなところなのだが、そこには電気がなく夜は真っ暗。一人が灯を掲げる中で、しめたばかりの鶏の羽根をみんなでむしった。1年ぶりに帰省したお姉ちゃんを迎え、家族親戚は大喜びだった。

Khasi family preparing a chicken for supper. Sister Firstly Mary is our first member of MMS from the Khasi tribe. Initially I have learned about Khasi culture little by little from them. One thing I noticed was that their girls' names are quite interesting. The name Mary is very common among Catholics. She, being the first child in her family, they put "Firstly" before Mary. Joyful Mary is another example. It was dark in the kitchen as there was no electricity. Her sister held up the lamp, the rest took off the feathers. The family was simply happy to have her big sister back after a long absence.

# クワイの物語──ある小屋での惨劇

カシ語でいう「クワイ」(呼び方は民族によって異なる)とは、ヤシ科の樹木ビンロウの実と少々の石灰をキンマの葉(パーン)で包んだもの。インドではパーンを噛むのはごく一般的な風習です。メガラヤ州に暮らす先住民族にとっても、噛みタバコのように用いるクワイは欠かせない伝統文化の一つ。おもてなしのシンボルとも言えるでしょう。

ビンロウはインド北東部各地で栽培されていて、カシヒルズ産は格段においしいことで知られています。そのせいでしょうか、カシ族ほどクワイを嗜む民族はいないかもしれません。大人たちは文字通り四六時中クワイを噛んでいるので、唇とその周りは赤く染まり、歯はお歯黒を塗ったかのようになっている人をよく見かけます。カシ族の女性は皆、ビンロウとパーン、ペースト状になった石灰の入った小さな入れ物と、ビンロウの皮を剥くためのナイフを入れた小型のバッグを肩から下げていて、いつでもどこでも誰とでもクワイを楽しめるように備えています。食事やお茶の後にも必ず登場する、このクワイにまつわる伝説があります。

昔々、カシヒルズのとある小さな村に、固い友情で結ばれた二人の男性が住んでいました。一人はニックという名の、何一つ不自由ない生活を送る裕福な独身男性。もう一人は極貧の労働者で妻帯者のシン。貧富の差こそありますが、二人はお互いをとても尊敬し合っていました。ニックは何かにつけてシンを家に呼び、帰る時には必ず手土産を持たせました。

ある時、シンはいつも招かれてばかりでは心苦しいと、妻のラックと相談してニックを招待することにしました。ところが、日時をきちんと決めていなかったものですから、いざニックが訪ねにきた時、家には一人分のお米すらなかったのです。ラックは慌ててご近所を頼りますが、分けてくれる人は誰もいませんでした。親友に食事すら提供できない屈辱のうち

に生きるより死んだほうがましだと、シンは台所にあった包丁で自らの命を絶ってしまいました。それを見たラックも、シンの胸に刺さったナイフを抜き取ると後を追ったのです。

シンがなかなか戻ってこないので、不審に思ったニックが台所に行くと、そこには血にまみれ息絶えた二人の変わり果てた姿がありました。何よりも大事な友人をこんなことで失い、ぼう然自失したニックは、同じナイフで自殺してしまいました。

夜が更けて、あたりはしんと静まり返っています。そこに何も知らない逃走中の泥棒がやってきて、これはちょうどいい隠れ家だと忍び込み、そのまま朝まで寝入ってしまいました。明るくなって目を覚まし、やっと惨状に気がついた泥棒は、誰かに見つかれば泥棒どころか3人の殺人犯として極刑に処せられるに違いないと恐怖におののき、自らの命を絶ってしまったのです。

すべての顛末を知った村の人たちは、これは誰にでも起こり得ることだと深く心配しました。そしてカシ族にとっての創造主(ウ・ブレイ)に祈りを捧げ、貧しい者のところに裕福な友人が訪れてもこんな悲劇が二度と起こらないために、お米よりも簡単に手に入る食べ物を恵んでくれるよう祈願したのです。

すべてをご存じの神様は、貧富の差があろうとも心置きなく交歓し、食事やお茶を出さなくてももてなすことができるようにと、4人の亡骸からビンロウとキンマと石灰とタバコをお造りになりました。そして、ニックはビンロウに、シンとラックはパーンと石灰に、そして泥棒は隠れることができるようにと口の端に入れるタバコに姿を変えたのです。それ以来、この4つを組み合わせたクワイを振る舞いながら一緒に時を過ごす習慣がカシ族の間で始まったということです。

Story of *Kwai*: Tragedy in a hut

*Kwai* is a Khasi term which refers to the combination of a neatly folded betel leaf (paan) smeared with soda lime and areca nut. It is quite a common custom in India to chew paan. For the tribal people in the state Meghalaya, it is one of the most important traditions and a symbol of their hospitality. Areca nuts are cultivated all over in the region of North East India, and the variety grown in Khasi Hills is especially tasty. Because of that, perhaps, the Khasi people seem to enjoy *Kwai* the most of everyone in the region. They chew it whenever they are awake, which makes people's mouth red and their teeth black. All Khasi women have a small bag hanging on their shoulder, in which they keep areca nuts, a small container of soda lime paste, betel leaves and a knife to skin the areca nuts so that they can enjoy *Kwai* at their convenience. It is also a custom, without fail, to offer *Kwai* after a meal or tea.

This is how the Khasi folklore explains how the *Kwai* tradition came about: A long time ago, in a village of Khasi Hills, there were two men tied to one another through a faithful friendship. One was a prosperous merchant who was single, named Nik. The other was a very poor laborer, married, who did all sorts of jobs to make ends meet, named Shing. Though they did not have much in common, they respected and appreciated each other. Nik used to invite Shing to his house every so often and treated him with utmost graciousness. Feeling terribly bad about this one-sided friendship, Shing decided this time he would invite Nik to his house. Unfortunately because they had not set a date for this special visit, when Nik came over, there was not enough rice even for one person. Lak, Shing's wife, went out to ask their neighbors to give them some rice in vain. Shing could not tolerate living in such shame and humiliation. Not being able to treat his precious friend, he killed himself with a kitchen knife. Lak followed him.

Wondering why Shing had left him alone, Nik came to the kitchen and found a dreadful site. He realized what happened to his dearest friend from such a trivial matter and struck with grief, he too decided to kill himself.

The night fell with a deep silence. Then came a thief search-
ing for a hiding place in the house and fell asleep there till
the next morning. When the fellow woke up and on seeing
the horrible scene, he was terrified that he would be blamed
and put to death or beaten up and so killed himself too.
The villagers were deeply moved with pity as they learned
about this terrible incident. They prayed to U Blei, the Khasi
God, and asked to create a product that was easier to procure
than rice so that such a tragedy would never happen again.
God, who knew everything, created a betel nut tree, a betel
leaf plant, lime and tobacco from the four bodies. Nik meta-
morphosed into a betel nut, Shing and Lak became the paan
and lime which are taken together, and the thief turned into
tobacco, which the Khasi insert in the corner of their mouths,
as if it were a hiding place. It is from this story that the custom of *Kwai* started among the Khasi.

[参考文献 | Bibliography]

Kynpham Sing Nongkynrih, *Around the Hearth: Khasi Legends*
(India: Penguin Books, 2007).

## リカイ──身投げの滝

カシヒルズの南にあるバングラデシュとの国境に近いチェラプンジは、いくつもの壮麗な滝があり、観光地として有名です。乾季が終わると滝を愛でにインド各地や海外から多くの人が訪れます。「ノ・カ・リカイ・フォールズ（リカイが身投げした滝）」もその一つ。名前の由来となった説話は、カシヒルズに伝わる数ある悲劇の中でもとりわけ悲しく、また残酷なものと言われています。

昔々、「暗黒の滝」と呼ばれる力強い大滝を見下ろすことができる村がありました。そこに住んでいたリカイという女性ほど不幸な星のもとに生まれた人はいないでしょう。両親と幼くして死に別れたリカイは遠い親戚に引き取られ、ひどく冷たくあしらわれ続けました。それにもかかわらず、彼女はたくましく、蘭のように美しく成人し、愛する男性と結ばれて娘を授かります。しかし、つかの間の幸せは夫の突然の死によって脆くも消え去ってしまいました。

身を粉にして働きながら愛娘を育て上げたリカイは、ずる賢い男にしつこく言い寄られ、とうとう再婚します。ところが、その男はリカイと娘に虐待の限りを尽くし、なんとリカイの留守中に娘を虐殺し、こともあろうにその娘の亡骸でスープを作り、帰宅したリカイに食べさせたのです！すべてを知ったリカイは半狂乱になり、こんな呪われた人生から抜け出すにはもう死ぬより他はないと、暗黒の滝に身を投げたのでした。

この惨劇の後、地元の神主によって浄めの儀式が執り行われました。この村は地の利が良く、農産物の売り買いと豊かに採れる鉄鉱石で大層栄えていたのですが、リカイの悲劇の後に住民たちは立ち退きを命じられ、村は消滅しました。人々はリカイの辿った悲運は経済的繁栄の影に潜む悪と心の破滅をあぶり出したかのようだと囁き合い、後世に言い伝えたのです。

Noh Ka Likai Falls

Cherrapunji is located in the southern part of West Khasi
Hills near the Bangladeshi border. The area is surrounded
with beautiful nature. When the dry season ends, many people come to enjoy the beauty from far and near. Noh Ka
Likai Falls are one of the attractive stops for visitors. The
name literally means "The Plunge of Ka Likai Falls" and
there is a tale behind it. They say it is one of the cruelest and
saddest of legends among the numerous tragedies of the
Khasi tribe.
Once upon a time, there was a village overlooking a powerful
soaring waterfall known as "The Dark Waterfall." A woman
named Likai lived in the village. Perhaps no one was more
unfortunate than she was. Her parents died when she was
still very young. According to Khasi folklore, her distant relatives had to look after her, but she was always treated without love. Despite this she had grown strong and blossomed
like an orchid. She then married a man who loved her sin-
cerely and a baby girl was born. However, the happy moments
did not last long as her husband died suddenly of a disease.
Likai worked day and night to raise her child and eventually
her life reached a tranquil state. One day, a cunning man
appeared in her life who approached her persistently. She
gave in to marry him only to find herself and her beloved
daughter horribly abused by him. At the end he slaughtered
her daughter while Likai was away and made soup from her
body. When she returned he had her eat it without realizing
the contents! After finding out the devastating truth, Likai
cried: "Death is the only true and constant comrade of my
wretched life!" She then dashed towards the cascading
waters and plunged headfirst into it, which would bear the
tragic burden of her name forever.
As terribly sad as the story is, the magnificent scenery of the
area I saw is surely a lasting memento of Likai's beauty.

マウカルワット村
Mawkyrwat village, ML
カシの家族。カシは女系社会。
Khasi family. The Khasi tribe is a matrilineal society.

P. 222
マウカルワット村
Mawkyrwat village, ML
紅茶を振る舞うカシの女性。
紅茶は甘くミルクなし。

Khasi woman serving tea.
Tea is sweet and served
without milk.

P. 223
チェラプンジ
Cherrapunji, ML

観光客相手に焼きトウモロコ
シを売るカシの女性。
Khasi woman selling roasted
sweet corns to tourists.

P. 224
チェラプンジ
Cherrapunji, ML
カシ独特のクヌップという編笠
を被って、タイルについたコケ
を削るカシの女性。
Khasi woman cleaning the
tiles, putting a cover called
*Knup* so that she does not
get wet from drizzling rain.

P. 225
マウブリ村
Mawbri village, ML
田植えを終え、クヌップを被っ
て畦道を歩くカシの男性。

Khasi man walking on a
ridgeway between rice fields
with *Knup*.

P. 226
マウカルワット村
Mawkyrwat village, ML
カシの子どもたち。
Khasi children.

P. 226
マウカルワット村
Mawkyrwat village, ML
カシ族はとにかく子だくさん。
Khasi people have a large family with lots of children.

P. 227
マウカルワット村
Mawkyrwat village, ML
カシの女性は寒くなるとチェックのショールを纏う。
Khasi women in their typical shawl in winter.

P. 227
スミット
Sumit, ML
女性は若くして結婚する場合が多く、母親がお姉さんに見えることもしばしば。
It is not unusual for a woman to get married at a young age. Sometimes mother looks like an elder sister of her eldest daughter.

P. 228
リアールバン村
Liarbang village, ML

村の学校の生徒と先生。
Students and teachers of a village school.

P. 229
マウブリ村
Mawbri village, ML
カシの子どもたち。
Khasi children.

P. 230–232
マウブリ村
Mawbri village, ML
晴れてシスターになり、家族と感謝のミサを捧げる二人のMMS。マウブリの村人はほぼ全員がカトリック信者。家族にとってはまるで結婚式のような特別な日だ。女性たちは一張羅に着替えてお化粧に余念がない。自分の娘が、姉妹が、姪が、修道女になるということがどれだけ誇らしいことなのか、少しわかったような気がした。この日のご馳走のために、牛、豚が一頭ずつ屠られ、加えて鶏と魚が用意され、もちろん内臓も血も全部使われた。夜が更けるにつれ、おじさんたちは地酒ですっかり酔っぱらって絶好調。なんだか懐かしい光景だった。

Two of our sisters' homecoming after their profession of the first vows as Medical Mission Sisters. Their families offered the Thanksgiving Mass at the parish in the village. As almost all the villagers are Catholic, many joined the memorable celebration like a marriage. I appreciated how special it is for them to have their daughter, sister, or niece as a nun.

WEAVING OF SPIRIT:
A JOURNEY INTO NORTH EAST INDIA

# あとがき

『いのち綾なす』に登場する人々の言語、文化、生活、歴史的背景は極めて多様性に富み、また複雑に入り組んでいます。それぞれの土地にしっかりと根付いた日々の暮らしにはいつも歌と踊りがあり、力強い色彩が溢れ、そこに私は大きな流れの中に紡がれるいのちを感じるのです。

この本を作り上げていく過程でわかったことがあります。まずは、インド北東部で交流を深めてきた人々について、いつの間にかあたかもすべてを知っているかのごとく話すようになっていたこと。自分の無知を知らないことはなんとおそろしいことかとあらためて痛感しました。また今回は、口伝えの文化が育まれてきた土地で見聞きしたことを文字にしようと試みたわけですが（それも日本語と英語の！）、それはまったく頭を抱える作業でした。私自身の聞く力と想像力をもって理解したことをお伝えするしかないと腹を括り、最善を尽くしたつもりです。もう一つは、ミッショナリーという自分の立ち位置についてあまりにナイーブだったということ。正しい答えがあるわけではないかもしれませんが、とても大きな事柄だと感じました。今後も活動に携わっていく上での宿題として考え祈り続けようと思います。

現在のコロナ禍における数少ないプラス面は、私たちが「一つの世界」に住んでいるという現実を体験していることかもしれません。それぞれにまるで別世界のように感じる場所にあっても、同じ時代に同じ地球に住まう者同士、私たちは確かにつながり響き合っている。『いのち綾なす』が今この時に、表現されるべくして表現された作品になったことを心から願っています。

2021年12月3日
聖フランシスコ・ザビエル（インドと日本の守護聖人）の祝日
東京にて

# Epilogue

The language, culture, lifestyle and historical background of the peoples in *Weaving of Spirit* are incredibly diverse and intricately intertwined. Their lives are firmly rooted on the ground and filled with song and dance, and one is immersed in powerful colors everywhere. Here, in this reality I sense Life woven endlessly in the Flow of Creation.

As I was engaged in making the book during the past several months, there were two important as well as painful lessons I learned through honest and sincere communications with those who helped me prepare the materials. Firstly, I became aware, once again, how I can carry an attitude of overconfidence in the sharing of my experience in North East India. To know my own ignorance is, indeed, the first step to learn! Secondly, I discovered *naïveté* in myself about being a missionary. A question rises: what does it mean to be a missionary? Perhaps there is not a right answer as such, but it seems to me a significant question to keep pondering.
Another challenge was to put the stories and experiences into scripts and sentences of Japanese and English. I have a habit of briefly jotting down what I have captured in my journals, and those records are my basic resources. Words, however, have limitations and so does translation. With the generous cooperation of the team, I did my best to convey as authentically as possible whatever I understood with my simple listening, imagination and intuition.

Like many others I have not been able to travel at all for the past two years due to the COVID-19 pandemic. In some ways, COVID has helped us experience that truly we live in "One World." Each of us inhabits a world familiar to ourselves but unknown to others. Yet we surely are connected and resonate with one another in our uniqueness and diversity as contemporaneous dwellers on Mother Earth. It is my humble hope that *Weaving of Spirit* may express what is meant to be expressed to each reader in the present moment of our time.

December 3, 2021
Feast of St. Francis Xavier, Patron of India and Japan
Tokyo

謝辞

この本が完成に至るまで、励まし、尽力を惜しまず、快く助けてくださった多くの方々に深く感謝申し上げます。とりわけ──

メディカル・ミッション・シスターズ（MMS）の後援組織である活動基金委員会への寄付を通して出版を応援してくださった方々、惜しみないお志をくださったアメリカン・フィールド・サービス（AFS）関係者の皆さま、石川直美さんと石川和男さんに。デザインと校正および編集、そして写真編集において最高度のプロの技術とあたたかな心で支えてくださった小池俊起さん、小野冬黄さん、梁瀬薫さん、ジャック・デ・メロさんに。ユニークな地図とイラストを作成してくださった長野亮之介さんに。真摯で絶大なる協力とアドバイスをくださったゴッドフリー・ヴィサル・タポ神父さま、ケトゥオラヴィ・マリナさん、南風島渉さんに。適切な情報を提供してくださった笠井亮平さんに。的確な助言をくれた宮井加寿美さんに。発売元となることを快諾してくださったオリエンス宗教研究所の関係者の皆さまに。身に余る心のこもった序文を寄せてくれたシスター・マリア・ホーナングと MMS インド北東部管区の念入りな歴史を提供してくれたシスター・レティチア・エアルテイルに。忍耐強く英文校正と編集をしてくれたシスター・ルーシー・クライン・ギビンク、シスター・ヘレン・レンベック、フランソワ・デ・メロさんに。いつも励まし協力してくれた家族に。姉妹愛のうちに絶え間なく支えてくれた MMS アメリカ管区と MMS インド北東部管区のシスターと志願者たちに。そして、最後になりましたが、いつでも私をあたたかく迎え入れてくれたインド北東部の人々に特別な想いを込めて。

『いのち綾なす──インド北東部への旅』は、海を越え国境を越えて躍動するチームワークの賜物に他なりません。このお恵みに神様への賛美と感謝を捧げます。

延江由美子

# Acknowledgement

I would like to express my deep gratitude to each and every one who has encouraged, supported and given me helping hands so willingly until the completion of the book, especially:

Medical Mission Sisters (MMS) Specified Funds Committee whose generous donors made it possible to publish the book; all the supporters from American Field Service (AFS) community and Mr. and Mrs. Kazuo and Naomi Ishikawa for their generous contribution; Mr. Toshiki Koike, Ms. Fuyuki Ono, Ms. Kaoru Yanase and Mr. Jacques De Mélo for their superb professional skills of design and editing and for their most kind and thought considerations; Mr. Ryonosuke Nagano for his fine and unique maps and illustrations; Rev. Fr. Godfrey Vilasàl Thapo, Ms. Ketuoravi-ii Marina and Mr. Wataru Haejima for their most sincere and incredible support and advice; Dr. Ryohei Kasai for his reliable information; Ms. Kasumi Miyai for her brilliant advice; Oriens Institute for Religious Research who are publishing the book in Japan; Sr. Maria Hornung for her heartfelt Foreword which is more than I deserve; Sr. Laetitia Aerthayil for her thorough writing on the MMS history of North East India; Sr. Lucy Klein-Gebbinck, Sr. Helen Lembeck and Mr. Francois De Mélo for their patient and thoughtful work of editing the English text; Sisters of MMS in Unit North America and Sisters and aspirants of MMS in Unit North East India for their loving constant support; my family for all their encouragement; and last but not least, the peoples of North East India who have always welcomed me in their midst with such open hearts.

*Weaving of Spirit: A Journey into North East India* is nothing but the fruit of excellent team work of so many across lands and oceans. I thank and praise God for this gracious gift.


Yumiko Nobue

延江由美子
Yumiko Nobue

1963年、東京都生まれ。高校3年生の夏から1年間、アメリカン・フィール
ド・サービス(AFS)の交換留学生としてニューヨーク州に滞在。1987年、
北海道大学大学院獣医学研究科修了。1992年、アメリカ・カトリック大
学看護学部卒業。1995年、メディカル・ミッション・システーズ(MMS)に
入会。アメリカ管区で養成を受け、様々な統合療法を習得。2000年、イ
ンド北部管区に派遣される。2007年、インド北東部管区に異動。その
後、2011年に活動拠点を東京に移してからはインド北東部についての
講演会や執筆、大学非常勤等に従事しながら、主にインド北東部やア
メリカ・フィラデルフィアを定期的に行き来してMMSの活動を続けてい
る。2015年に写真集『Moving Cloud Flowing Water: A Journey Into
North East India』(邦題=行雲流水——インド北東部への旅)を出版。

Yumiko Nobue was born and raised in Tokyo, Japan. At the age of 18,
she spent one year as an American Field Service (AFS) exchange school
student in New York state. She graduated from Hokkaido University
in Sapporo in 1987 with a masters degree in veterinary medicine.
Yumiko returned to USA in 1989, completing a degree in nursing at
Catholic University of America in 1992. She joined Medical Mission
Sisters (MMS) in Philadelphia in 1995. In her first years with MMS,
she studied massage and other healing arts. In 2000, she was assigned
to North India Province and in 2007 was transferred to North East
India Province. In 2011 Yumiko shifted her base to Tokyo with her
primary mission involvements shared between Japan and North East
India under the umbrella of North America Province. An avid amateur
photographer, Yumiko captured images of life in North East India
which were published as a pictorial memoir, *Moving Cloud Flowing
Water: A Journey Into North East India* in 2015.

参考文献
Bibliography

S. Woodburn Kirby, *The War Against Japan, Vol. III: The Decisive Battles* (HMSO, 1962).

中根千枝『未開の顔・文明の顔』中央公論新社、1990年

多良俊照『入門ナガランド インド北東部と先住民を知るために』社会評論社、1998年

T. B. Subba and G. C. Ghosh, *The Anthropology of North-East India: A Textbook* (India: Orient Longman, 2003).

Kynpham Sing Nongkynrih, *Around the Hearth: Khasi Legends* (India: Penguin Books, 2007).

南風島渉「ナガランド 国家・国境の意味を探る旅」『見えないアジアを歩く』(見えないアジアを歩く編集委員会編著)三一書房、2008年

カカ・D・イラル『血と涙のナガランド──語ることを許されなかった民族の物語』(木村真希子・南風島渉訳[日本語抄訳])コモンズ、2011年

『南を考える13 ナガランド──私たちが歩いた紛争地』明治学院大学国際平和研究所、2011年

森田勇造『写真で見るアジアの少数民族3 南アジア編』三和書籍、2012年

いのち綾なす──インド北東部への旅
Weaving of Spirit: A Journey into North East India

2021年12月25日
初版発行

First published in
December 25, 2021

編著
延江由美子

Author and Editor
Yumiko Nobue

監修
梁瀬薫

Supervisor
Kaoru Yanase

寄稿
マリア・ホーナング
レティチア・エアルテイル

Contribution
Maria Hornung
Laetitia Aerthayil

校正
小野冬黄

Japanese Proofreading
Fuyuki Ono

英文校正
ルーシー・クライン・ギビンク
ヘレン・レンベック

English Proofreading
Lucy Klein-Gebbinck
Helen Lembeck

写真編集
ジャック・デ・メロ

Photo Editor
Jacques De Mélo

イラスト
長野亮之介

Illustration
Ryonosuke Nagano

デザイン
小池俊起

Design
Toshiki Koike

写真提供
小池俊起
cover, p.008–009, 012, 019,
033, 129, 169, 209
メディカル・ミッション・シスターズ
p.022, 254

Photo Courtesy
Toshiki Koike
cover, p.008–009, 012, 019,
033, 129, 169, 209
Medical Mission Sisters
p.022, 254

印刷
株式会社八紘美術

Printing
Hakkou Art Co., Ltd.

発行
メディカル・ミッション・シスターズ

発売
オリエンス宗教研究所

Publisher
Medical Mission Sisters
8400 Pine Road
Philadelphia, PA 19111 USA

Distribution
Oriens Institute for
Religious Research

オリエンス宗教研究所

代表：C. コンニ
〒156-0043
東京都世田谷区松原2-28-5
Tel 03-3322-7601
Fax 03-3325-5322
https://www.oriens.or.jp/